Lessons for Life 2

Lessons for Life 2

Jill Masters

THE WAKEMAN TRUST, LONDON

LESSONS FOR LIFE 2

©Jill Masters 1992
First published 1992

THE WAKEMAN TRUST
Elephant & Castle
London SE1 6SD

ISBN 1 870855 11 6

Cover design by Andrew Sides

Visual aid drawings by Alan MacGregor
with graphics and presentation by Andrew Owen

Scripture quotations not otherwise identified are from the New American Standard Bible, ©The Lockman Foundation 1960, 1962, 1963, 1968, 1971, 1972, 1973, 1974, 1975, 1977.

Printed in Great Britain by Mackays of Chatham.

CONTENTS
Book 2

INTRODUCTION

Book Two of *Lessons for Life* now follows the most encouraging reception of Book One, providing the second year of a four-year syllabus. Details of the whole four-year scheme appear on pages 206-207. Take-home leaflets for scholars together with other helps for teachers are available for use with *Lessons for Life*. (The address for enquiries is shown on page 207.)

From the Introduction to Lessons for Life 1:—

These lesson notes have an evangelistic aim, using selected Bible portions which are clearly intended for evangelistic application. Each lesson seeks to confront children with a true understanding of truths and arguments which, under the Holy Spirit, could lead to conversion.

Alongside this, they are intended to give a good outline knowledge of all the Scriptures. The syllabus seeks to deal with Bible events in an orderly manner, worthy of the Word of God. The Old Testament is mainly dealt with chronologically, so that the pattern of God's dealings with mankind before Christ are known and appreciated. In this lesson scheme, the Old Testament lessons are interleaved with the Gospels and *Acts*. Both children and teachers prefer this method of following a basic historical pattern, to those approaches with jump from one part of the Bible to another with such frequency that all perspective is lost. Each week this scheme provides another instalment in the great plan of God. Pastoral needs of young believers can be catered for, so that parents (unbelievers as well as believers) will appreciate that their children are receiving a biblical education.

The third aim of these notes is to present vital spiritual topics to the minds of the young. The plan of the Bible itself suggests various themes which should be highlighted in our teaching.

By this means we aim to offer the children a great and varied Gospel challenge as they set out on life's journey. Prayerfully, our concern is that it will lead them to the Saviour in early years, but if not, it will plant in their minds and hearts a knowledge of the Lord which can be used by His Spirit in later years to prick their consciences and lead them to seek the Saviour.

Experience has shown that teachers are the best people to adapt the lessons to an individual class. These notes therefore contain material which can be adapted to the needs of all age groups, from Beginners (pre-school age) to the teenage Bible Class. A range of suggested applications and guidelines are provided so that teachers may utilise the particular points most suited to their age group. Older classes often use the complete lesson outline, while younger classes select fewer points. In the many years this scheme has been in use, no teacher has ever complained that this has presented a problem.

This lesson system is tailored to fit around the Sunday School year. Most Sunday Schools, like day schools, will divide their programme into three terms a year. Most will want to break off from regular lessons for Christmas, New Year, Easter and other holidays and special occasions. Speakers usually choose and prepare their own subject on these Sundays, and it is assumed, therefore, that a maximum of 46 lessons per year is required. The lessons are grouped into series, and individual Sunday Schools may use these in any order to suit their Sunday School year. However, the Old Testament series should be kept in chronological order, whereas New Testament series may be fitted into the year according to choice.

The promise of the Lord that His Word will not return to Him empty (*Isaiah 55.11*) proves a great incentive to continue through days of patient toil. Slowly and surely the satisfaction of watching God's Word taking effect in the lives and behaviour of young children confirms its truthfulness. In days of irreligion and apathy amongst the adult population, it is extremely touching to witness large numbers of children gathering together, and to see the Lord still preparing His praise out of the mouths of infants (*Matthew 21.16*).

He who goes to and fro weeping, carrying his bag of seed, shall indeed come again with a shout of joy, bringing his sheaves with him (Psalm 126.6).

Series 7
Exodus – Joshua (Part I)
The Christian Pilgrimage –
SALVATION FROM SIN'S SLAVERY

47 – Slavery in Egypt
After almost four hundred years in Egypt the Hebrews have become a nation of slaves under the tyrant Pharaoh. God plans to release them and His plan begins with a baby.

48 – Moses' Choice
Moses stands to inherit the throne of Egypt, yet he chooses to suffer affliction with his own people. Why?

49 – God Calls to Moses
Many years later, in a far-off land, Moses is surprised to see the burning bush and to hear what the Lord has planned. God has similar surprises for us.

50 – Resisting the Lord
On nine separate occasions God sends an awful plague, yet Pharaoh will not heed the warnings. How does God warn us today?

51 – Redeemed!
At last the slaves are free, but what is the price? We too must be redeemed with 'precious blood'.

52 – Guidance
God sends a fiery, cloudy pillar to lead the way, and the

Israelites begin their pilgrimage. On our journey through life, will we be the victims of chance, boredom and misery, or will we look to the Lord to be our Guide?

53 – Protection

God performs a mighty miracle at the Red Sea which enables the people of Israel to step out of Egypt into a land of freedom. How does God deliver us from the kingdom of darkness into the kingdom of His dear Son?

54 – Provision

Two million mouths to feed in a wilderness – a big problem for Moses – but soon God provides all their needs in miraculous ways. Life is full of wonderful experiences and remarkable adventures for all who trust the Lord.

Teachers' Introduction to the Series

The book of *Exodus* is a truly remarkable book which, as Sunday School teachers, we should look forward to teaching with great anticipation. Within its forty chapters we see the great 'I AM WHO I AM' speaking to and dealing with people like ourselves, and we know that these events are full of direction for us. Below are listed just some of the outstanding features of the book which will be focused upon in the lessons.

(1) **The Gospel.** It is a book full of the Gospel. In numerous incidents God taught His ancient people the way in which He saves men and women from the influences which enslave them. These events, characterised by drama and variety, will remain indelibly stamped on the mind from childhood to old age. The principles taught remain unaltered to provide rich Gospel material for our weekly lessons.

(2) **Warnings.** It is a book full of warnings. It shows how even the Israelites who had witnessed the mighty acts of God frequently hardened their hearts and refused God's love. From these events we can demonstrate the continuing unreasonableness of unbelief.

(3) **A pilgrimage.** The book's overall picture of a people set free from Pharaoh and taken on a pilgrimage through the wilderness to the promised land, is a wonderful illustration of the Christian pilgrimage through this earthly life to Heaven.

While we must be careful to avoid giving the impression that all Israelites were believers, it is possible to see *Exodus* as the Scripture's own *Pilgrim's Progress*. This overall theme provides a cohesion to the series which is always extremely helpful in the teaching of children.

(4) Moses. The book of *Exodus* gives us a wonderful portrait of the man Moses, who bore enormous burdens and responsibilities, and of whom it is written, *the Lord used to speak to Moses face to face, just as a man speaks to his friend (Exodus 33.11)*.

Visual Aid

VA 1 (see page 13) is designed for use throughout this series to remind children of the overall theme of a journey or pilgrimage.

Slavery in Egypt (47)
The Birth of Moses

Exodus 1 – 2.10 *April 20. 08*

Aim: To use the slavery of the Israelites to illustrate our own bondage under sin. To point out that in both situations it was God Who took the initiative and put into operation His plan for release.

Lesson Outline

Open the lesson by describing the slavery into which the Israelites had fallen. Describe what life was like for the children of slaves. Show pictures of slave teams being used to build the pyramids. Go on to explain, under the following headings, that there was much more to their suffering than the physical rigours which the Egyptians forced upon them.

(1) They were 'sold'. The Israelites had sold their freedom. In return for promises of food, shelter and security they had sold their valuables (perhaps these included heirlooms brought by their families from Canaan) and finally they were reduced to surrendering themselves.

Surprise the children by suggesting that there is a sense in which we are slaves too — slaves to sin and Satan. Draw parallels between the situation in Egypt and our own.

Show how we surrender our 'possessions' to the enemy of our souls. Sin promises to give us happiness, enlightenment and fulfilment. In return we 'sell' to Satan our hearts, our minds, and in the end ourselves. (Give examples to younger children, eg: sin suggests that lying will do us no harm and get us easy gain, but instead it takes away our integrity.) Gradually we give away all that is worthy. Like a corrupt money-lender who demands the last penny from his victims, sin sucks every virtue from us.

(2) **No choice.** The Israelites were now living in little hovels with nothing to call their own. Daily they were herded together and driven like animals to their place of work. They were forced to haul huge stones across the desert in the hot sun, and if they complained or asked for so much as a drink, they would be given more to do, and whipped. If their taskmasters demanded higher productivity they had no choice but to supply their demands. They had no rights, no option.

As we get older, sin grows stronger. Sin, which at one time we only toyed with, gets a hold on us, as drink gets hold of an alcoholic. Sometimes we want to live better lives, but we discover that we have no choice or power to do so. Sin is now our master. Children who were born to slaves realised with horror that they must follow the way of their parents. So must we, for we are all born sinners.

(3) **No freedom.** The slaves were never free. Later they asked to have three days leave and were refused. They could never enjoy improving their own homes, going on holiday, or making new friends. Their life was one long round of labour and toil, with its boundaries strictly drawn by the Egyptians.

Explain that this is how sin treats *us*. It robs us of all that is best in life. It restricts our experience to the physical and mundane side of life. Unbelievers never see the best things; never experience real joy and fulfilment. Just as the Israelites were never able to explore beyond their workplace, so sin prevents us from seeing outside of flesh and time: in other words we never experience *spiritual* things, such as feeling and tasting the presence, power and kindness of the Lord in our lives.

(4) **No help.** The Israelites had no hope of help to secure their

Copy the three drawings onto card or thick
paper. Then cut and fold as shown so that only
one face is visible. As Egypt is explained, the
small flap at the bottom can be unfolded to
apply the meaning. Do the same with each section.

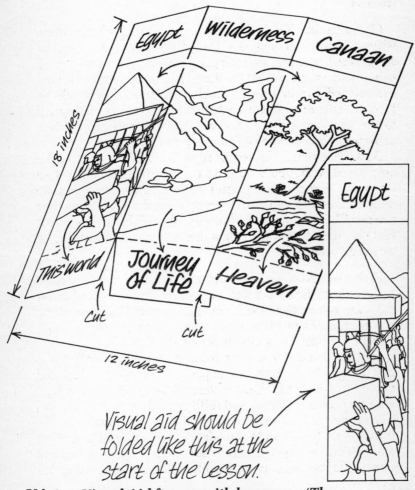

Visual aid should be
folded like this at the
start of the lesson.

**VA 1 – Visual Aid for use with lessons on 'The
Christian Pilgrimage'.**

freedom. They had no weapons or money of their own, and no friendly nation to set them free. They were entirely at the mercy of the Egyptians. The most they could hope for was to be kept alive as long as they worked hard.

Satan makes it very difficult for his slaves to escape. He makes us weak; he burdens us with his work, and he blinds our minds to any possible source of help. If ever we feel the longing to be free, he puts doubts and unbelief into our minds. Ask the children if they have ever tried to turn over a new leaf and live a good life. Tell them how Martin Luther tried and failed in his early years. Remind them that in this world there are many specialists in all kinds of subjects, but no one, including doctors or teachers, can help anyone eradicate sin!

(5) No will. After a number of years in this state, the *will* of the people was broken too. They were so trained to obey orders that they forgot how to think for themselves. Like people who have served long terms in an institution or in prison, they became dependent on their taskmasters. They did not cry to God for help for many years yet.

Sin does this to us. We become dependent on our sin. We cannot imagine how we can live without all our pride and selfishness and especially our sinful pleasures, and so we fear getting free from sin. This is why so many people are afraid to go to church. Even very old people staring death in the face are still reluctant to turn to the Saviour. Sin is so much of a habit, they dare not leave it behind. They prefer to sit in the squalor of sin than be washed clean. Ask the class how far they have come to be ruled by sin, and satisfied with its narrow ways.

(6) Payment – death! Finally Pharaoh, alarmed at the number of Hebrews, ordered the death of all their baby sons. Death – on a terrible scale – struck the nation. Help the class to share the horror of this edict. Help them to imagine the feelings which filled a Hebrew family when a little boy was born, the natural joy overwhelmed by the horror of handing him to the soldiers to be drowned. Describe how this affected the parents, snatching away all hopes of a better future.

Show how the wages of sin is death. Instead of rewarding us for a life of service, Satan's final aim is to see our exhausted, aged bodies die, and then to see our souls consigned to hell for eternity.

God's work. Describe how God began to act in this situation. Before receiving any plea from them, God took pity upon His people and began to carry out His plan. How? We might expect Him to use another powerful nation to invade Egypt and release the slaves. Instead He looked down on that land and used a weak, helpless, threatened baby to begin His purpose of deliverance. Briefly relate the events of Moses' escape from death. Most children are very familiar with his rescue from the ark of bulrushes hidden in the Nile. Never refer to this as a 'story' because we want to convince the children of the truth of God's Word, and the word 'story' is usually linked with fairy-tales.

Give a hint of the future shape of events. Moses was protected and provided for by the Lord in an amazing way so that the people would learn that only God could save them. It was not until Moses was an old man, forgotten by the Israelites and hated by the Egyptians, that the Lord sent him to deliver Israel.

Explain to the class that becoming a Christian is like waking up and realising you have been living in a dark prison, chained up by Satan, and unable to experience life 'outside' – ie: *spiritual* life. The years of imprisonment have left you weak and emaciated and you have no hope of escape. Suddenly there walks into the cell a person with the equipment to cut your chains, a torch to show you the way out, and a firm hand to support you. While you had been dreaming, he had been busy planning and enacting your rescue. Ask Who this Person might be. Urge your class to wake up, see their true position and turn to the Saviour Who is willing to release them and set them on the road to Heaven. Urge them to come along next week so that they can learn how God's great plan was carried out and how the Israelites were freed to begin their great journey to a new and better land.

Moses' Choice (48)
Moses Has to Leave Egypt

Exodus 2.11-15; Hebrews 11.24-27

Aim: To apply the lesson of *Hebrews 11* to our children: *By faith Moses, when he had grown up, refused to be called the son of Pharaoh's daughter; choosing rather to endure ill-treatment with the*

*people of God, than to enjoy the passing pleasures of sin; considering
the reproach of Christ greater riches than the treasures of Egypt; for
he was looking to the reward.*

Lesson Outline

Moses' choice –

(1) **Ease.** Tell the class how most people, given the privileged
position of Moses in the Egyptian palace, would have stayed
just where they were. They would have remained loyal to
whatever guaranteed them a life of ease and pleasure. They
would not have stirred their consciences or troubled their
thoughts about their poor and oppressed countrymen.

Children are often the same. When they start out in life they
are drawn irresistibly to the place or person who has most to
offer them and they do not want to change in any way. The Lord
Jesus warned that if we are to find eternal life we must leave the
broad, easy way and move to the narrow, unpopular road.
Challenge the class to consider whether they are trapped in a
kind of net, living just as they have always lived, and never
considering any change to be necessary.

(2) **Riches.** Unlike many of us, Moses stood to enjoy a life of
wealth and prosperity. As the son of the princess he was very
spoilt, and well-placed for the future. We know from the
interior of the pyramids that the Egyptian royal family enjoyed
very great riches and splendour. Would anyone in their right
mind consider throwing away such riches?

(3) **Power.** One might become bored even by riches, but
Moses was given every opportunity for intellectual satisfaction
as well. The Egyptians were very skilled in all kinds of
interesting sciences, and Moses had the privilege of learning
them all. His education was not merely academic but *applied*.
He could design things, organise any scheme or project he
wanted to, engage in intriguing research, and so on. He could
tour the empire, visit the great sights, and either do worthwhile
things or just play and have fun. He could do anything he
wanted to do. He may well have been destined to become a
Pharaoh himself, but in any case he was trained to exercise
power and leadership. Ambition has a strong hold on many
people. Would Moses have the will to throw away these

Moses' choice

EITHER ___   OR ___

Power

Glory

Influence

Suffering

Affliction

But for a Season | But with God's people

Take a large sheet of card and draw the pictures above. Write the words as shown. Cut a slit at the bottom and fold the flaps up so they are hidden.

As the lesson proceeds, and once you have described the choice Moses was faced with, unfold the flaps to make the application.

VA 2 – Visual Aid for use with Lesson 48 – 'Moses' Choice'.

dazzling prospects?

Point out that it ought to be easier for us to turn aside from the world's allurements, yet we too are gripped by the desire to be successful and influential. Even children put their anxiety to be popular, and to get benefits now, before giving serious consideration to the Lord's claim upon their lives.

The alternative. Describe how Moses' peace of mind was spoilt. Despite his magnificent surroundings he knew that he was a Hebrew, and so he thought about the teachings of God and how he should serve the Lord God. Whenever Moses visited the newly-built store cities he knew that it was his own flesh and blood who had built them under conditions of terrible slavery. He felt uneasy when he returned to enjoy the luxury of palace life knowing that by birth he should have been amongst them. To whom did he belong? The question arose in his mind — was he an Egyptian or a Hebrew? Suppose he were to return to the Hebrews, what would it mean to him?

(1) **A hard decision.** It would mean taking a very big decision. Few would relish the prospect. It would mean a very big change and it would mean leaving behind the life to which he had grown accustomed. All who become Christians have to experience a great change when they are converted. They have to open their minds to a whole new way of life. Instead of living for self, they will be living for the Lord.

(2) **Poverty.** Moses would have to leave behind the fabulously rich palace and make his way to the hovels which the Hebrews accepted as their homes, and share their hardship. All the possessions he had proudly acquired would have to go.

When people become Christians they have to leave their pride and worldly ambitions behind as they go to the Lord Jesus and humbly ask for His forgiveness and converting power to be extended to them.

(3) **Reproach.** Instead of being waited upon and obeyed, Moses might well become not just a servant but probably a hunted or victimised person. All those who follow Jesus must be willing to bear persecution. The Christian life is not easy. Many people who reject the Lord are against Christians and dislike them and try to harm them in some way or other.

Ask the class what their choice would be. Strangely, Moses made a most unexpected decision. He chose to see himself as a Hebrew. He refused to be called the son of Pharaoh's daughter. Why? Whatever caused him to renounce all the advantages which lay before him?

Greater riches. Moses realised that the glories of Egypt would last only for his lifetime; that they were *passing pleasures*. What did all these riches amount to anyway? Would they ease his conscience? Could they make him happy? Might they not be snatched away at a moment's notice? Could he take them with him when he died? Moses saw how short-lived these Egyptian splendours were. He also knew that they did not even make the members of the royal household happy.

God's people. On the other hand, he began to think deeply. Who were these ill-treated Hebrews? Were they not the Lord's people? Though they were living in bondage now, had not God promised to set them free and give them a country of their own? Those among them who truly loved the Lord had been promised a home in Heaven far more splendid than any Egyptian palace; a home which would never fade away, but which had been prepared for them by the Lord Himself. What riches! Moses thought of his *real* mother. Though she was a slave, yet she knew the Lord. She was a daughter of the King of Heaven.

As Moses considered this last factor, he saw that he could gladly forgo the short-lived treasures of Egypt for the riches of being numbered among God's children and of knowing Him and being a part of His great plan.

Moses visits his people. Summarise the events which showed where Moses' choice had taken him – his identification with the Hebrew slave to the extent of killing the Egyptian. Show that his action soon resulted in his being compelled to flee from Egypt (not because he was afraid of Pharaoh but because he knew he must keep his life, in order that one day he might return to free the Israelites). He had exchanged the life of a prince for that of a shepherd. But God never lets our love for Him go unnoticed and in the next lesson we shall see how He honoured Moses.

Our choice. Ask the class if they have ever given any serious consideration to this matter. Remind them that it is the most important issue they will ever have to think about. Warn them not to be deceived by the fleeting pleasures of sin. If they find this hard, urge them to pray to the Lord and ask Him to open their eyes to the things which really matter, the things which are real and eternal. Jesus Himself pleaded with people to forsake the treasures of earth which rust and decay, and to put their treasure in Heaven (see *Matthew 6.19-20*). Millions of people have done just that and not one of them has been disappointed. Even while living on earth, with the joys of Heaven still before them, they can say: —

> *Saviour, if of Zion's city,*
> *I through grace a member am,*
> *Let the world deride or pity,*
> *I will glory in Thy name:*
> *Fading is the worldling's pleasure,*
> *All his boasted pomp and show!*
> *Solid joys and lasting treasure,*
> *None but Zion's children know.*

Visual Aid

VA 2 (see page 17) will help to show in graphic terms the choice which confronted Moses.

God Calls to Moses (49)
The Burning Bush

Exodus 3 – 4.5   5/4/ 0??

Aim: To take four simple but all-important Gospel 'surprises' to show the way of salvation.

Lesson Outline

Tell the class that it was now forty years since Moses had made his fateful choice to be counted as one of the Lord's people rather than to claim all the wealth and power which he could have enjoyed as 'grandson' of Pharaoh. His lifestyle had changed considerably. Far away from the bustling life of Egypt's capital, Moses had spent many years in the lonely desert minding his father-in-law's sheep.

As a highly-educated man, fully familiar with the military science of the day, he must have debated in his mind all possible means of releasing his fellow-Israelites from slavery, and come to the firm conclusion that, humanly speaking, the task was impossible. Perhaps he occasionally received news from Egypt. Far from conditions improving for the Israelites, a new king had come to the throne who so oppressed them that they cried out in despair for relief.

An amazing sight. Perhaps one day Moses was reflecting on these sombre circumstances when his attention was caught by a flaming bush in the desert. As he looked, he saw something astonishing, because though the flames blazed fiercely, the bush remained intact and undamaged. As the fire continued, unable to harm the bush and to burn itself out, Moses turned aside to investigate. Then, to his utter amazement, he heard his own name being called from the bush.

Intrigue the children by suggesting that there are some big surprises in store for those who become Christians and walk with the Lord. God will speak to their hearts in a way which will startle and surprise them. He will not speak (as He did to Moses) with an audible voice, but He will speak to their hearts and minds in a remarkable way through His Word. Give the following examples based on Moses' experience at Horeb: –

Surprise 1 – God is alive and sees all. Many people today boast that they are atheists. They claim that there is no evidence or need for God and therefore assume that He can be ignored. Even many people who say that they believe in God seem to think that He is a weak, distant God Who does not care much about man's sin and will not do anything about it.

It often comes to us as a great shock to discover that the Lord is a *living* God, Who is *all-powerful*, *all-seeing* and *eternal*. Just as Moses received a shock as he heard his name called from that burning bush and realised that God was alive, and watching all that was going on, so we who think that God is remote and unseeing are surprised when we first realise that the Bible teaches that God sees us and knows everything about us. He is a *living* God!

Surprise 2 – We are not fit to approach God. Describe how Moses, full of curiosity, went closer to the burning bush, but as he did so, God told him to stop and first take off his shoes as a sign of great reverence for the holy and all-powerful God. Moses had to understand that on that very piece of ground he was to meet God and that he needed to be filled with awe and humility.

We too must understand that the Lord is a holy God. This sometimes comes as a surprise because we constantly hear God's name used as a swear-word, and so many people seem to have no respect for Him at all. But when God 'communicates' with us by moving in our hearts (as we hear His Word) we suddenly realise with awe that He is great and holy, and that we are sinful, guilty people.

Before this happens we have no shame for our sins. Just as the Lord had to caution Moses, so He works in our hearts to make us feel that we are unclean and unacceptable as we are. Like Moses we then feel we want to hide, and we are humbled in the presence of God. The things we say and do seem ugly and unclean, and we realise that God has seen it all, and hates our sin.

Surprise 3 – God has a mighty plan to save us. As Moses stood there, conscious of his unworthiness in the presence of God, the Lord began to tell him great and wonderful things about how the Israelites would be delivered from captivity. He assured Moses that He was the God of Abraham, Isaac, and Jacob and that the time had now come for Him to free His people from Pharaoh. He had seen their misery, and would not only rescue them from their taskmasters, but would take them to a beautiful and fertile land.

In just the same way, when we come near to God, He not only shows us our sinfulness and unworthiness, but He shows us (in the Bible) His mighty plan to set us free and give us a new life. God's plan never fails to surprise us because it is something which we would never have thought of ourselves. When we begin to listen to God's Word in a spirit of respect and reverence, we really *hear* the Gospel message – that we, who are hell-deserving sinners, may come to experience His wonderful mercy and love. The Gospel tells us that though the Lord Jesus knew we would grow up as rebels far from Him and deeply involved in sin, He took action to save us by coming down to earth to be our substitute sin-bearer. Long before we turned to

Him with our first earnest prayer, the Lord Jesus died on Calvary's cross to pay the penalty of sin for those who trust in Him. Because He paid that price, we may be pardoned and given a new life.

Many people assume that they must earn their way to Heaven by good deeds. But the Gospel message says the opposite. It tells us that it is impossible for us to win God's favour, because we are too sinful, and that eternal life must come as a free gift from the Lord. The way to Heaven is by trusting in the Lord Jesus and what He has done on our behalf.

Describe how shocked the monk Martin Luther was, when as a person trying to earn God's favour by penances and fasting, he suddenly saw the message of the Gospel in the letter to the *Romans*. He realised in a flash that all his attempts to please God by inflicting punishments on himself were foolish and useless. Only Jesus Christ could save him from hell, because He had already suffered the most terrible punishment for every sin he had ever committed. So, Martin Luther realised that he had to receive forgiveness as a free gift. How pleased he was to make this surprising discovery! Ask the class if they have ever realised that God so loved them that He sent His only Son to die, so that if they truly believe in Him, they might be saved from all their sin.

Surprise 4 – God's power can be experienced in our lives. (There is no need for teachers to go into all the details of chapter 4. We shall only summarise Moses' qualms and the Lord's reassurances so as to continue our Gospel theme.) Moses knew only too well that the mission on which God was sending him was humanly impossible, and he voiced his fears to the Lord. God's answer was simple – 'But *I* will be with you.'

Some of our children may be daunted by the prospect of being converted, and be filled with doubts (just as Moses was about rescuing the children of Israel from Egypt). It seems all so unlikely to them that they could be freely pardoned and given a completely new life with an experience of God. Remind them that it is impossible for us to bring this about (just as it would have been impossible for Moses, an elderly shepherd, to liberate a whole nation single-handed). But it is possible with God, Whose power is unlimited and Who has *promised* to save those who come to Him. If God could rescue two million

Israelite slaves from the grip of the world's most powerful army, He can just as easily rescue us from Satan.

Tell the class how Moses doubted that the people would believe that God had spoken with him *(Exodus 4.1-5)*. So God enabled Moses to perform some miraculous deeds to prove that he really had the all-powerful God with him. These signs would convince the people, but they also greatly encouraged Moses!

The Lord does not give Christians the power to do miraculous things today — that was reserved for the men who gave the Scriptures — but we have a similar surprise to that of Moses when we come to Christ.

When we repent of sin and yield to the Lord, how do we know if we have really been converted? We are surprised at what happens to us. It is like a miracle! We find we love the Lord and want to worship Him. Our consciences come to life, and we deeply regret our sin, and we want to please the Lord. The Bible means very much more to us and it is far easier to understand. We somehow know we are children of God, and we discover we can pray. Also, we find we have much greater power over our sins, and at times (especially when we pray) we are aware that our Saviour is near to us. Just as Moses experienced God's power in a very surprising way, so do we when we truly come to God. It is God's way of proving that He has really blessed us.

Visual Aid

Obtain four pieces of card (large enough for your class to see) coloured red, orange, yellow and black on one side and white on the other. Cut each into the shape of a flame. (Edge each of the white sides with the colour of its reverse side.) On each of the white sides write one of the four surprises. Then draw the branches of a bush on either side of each piece of card (taking care not to draw through the words). Start the lesson with the four coloured flames arranged so as to form the outline of the burning bush. Then as you tell how Moses went to investigate, turn each flame round to emphasise your point. The children will be curious to discover what is written on the back of each flame. This visual presentation will help them remember the lesson.

5 / 1 1 / 0 8

Resisting the Lord (50)
The Ten Plagues

Exodus 5 – 10; Romans 9.17-18

Aim: To use the plagues, as the Lord intended, to proclaim His name through all the earth *(Exodus 9.16)*, and to warn the children of the great danger involved when they harden their hearts against the Lord.

Teachers' Introduction

If this lesson is to be profitable it needs to be well prepared. Careful reading of the passage indicates that each plague has a special lesson to teach. At each warning Pharaoh took another step downwards to disaster.

Lesson Outline

The first approach. Describe how Moses and Aaron delivered the Lord's demand to Pharaoh – *Let My people go.* The initial request was very reasonable. They asked only that the slaves should have three days 'holiday' so that they could go into the wilderness to hold a feast to the Lord. But Pharaoh's pride and heartlessness were immediately inflamed and he said, *Who is the Lord that I should obey His voice? (Exodus 5.2.)*

Explain to the class that we are little better. When we first hear God's commands our reaction is often, 'Why should I listen to God? Why should He interfere with my life?'

Proud and smug. Pharaoh reacted with characteristic spite. He would teach these Israelites! He would show them that Moses was their enemy and not their friend, so he commanded that from that time on, their task would be much harder – explain how. No doubt he felt very satisfied as reports came in that the slaves had bitterly complained against Moses. Our world is still filled with adults and children who criticise and dismiss the Lord.

Then God proceeded to set the children of Israel free from Pharaoh altogether, sending Moses and Aaron nine times to Pharaoh with nine terrible warnings, each more serious than the last. Each time Pharaoh refused to listen (or went back on

Take a large sheet of card and draw the staircase as shown. Copy the drawings opposite and place in position as the lesson proceeds. You may like to cover the wording & reveal as you go.

A battle within
– will he
listen to God?

He'll be sorry – but
only for a while!

Hard trials are sent to
bring him back to God –
but he still won't listen.

He'll listen to God
– if God will help him.

Refusing God becomes a
habit which he can't break.

He doesn't care how much pain his
stubbornness inflicts on others.

All the pleasures he puts before the Lord
fade away, but he still refuses God.

Judgement stares him in the face – but still all he
cares about are his treasures in this world.

Even at the eleventh hour God graciously offers to save,
but all he can do is curse the Lord and His messengers.

After so many gracious calls and opportunities, the
Lord must in the end be just and punish sin.

Ten Steps down to HELL

**VA 3 – Visual Aid for use with Lesson 50 –
'Resisting the Lord'.**

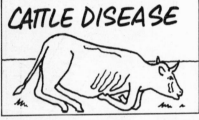

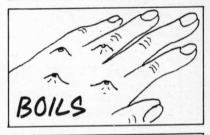

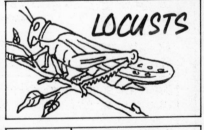

his word), his heart grew harder and his punishment more inevitable.

(1) The Nile turned to blood (*Exodus 7.14-25*). Before very long Moses and Aaron returned to Pharaoh. After warning him, Aaron lifted his rod so that the Nile, on which the land of Egypt depended, was turned to blood. So, the river which brought life to the land of Egypt, and which was worshipped by the Egyptians, was made foul. Instead of giving life it brought death. Imagine the battle that went on in Pharaoh's mind. On the one hand, he was revolted and horrified by this sight, realising both the economic consequences and the demoralising effect. On the other hand, he was determined not to be affected by any demonstration of God's power.

Young people well understand this struggle. Often they are challenged by their own wrongdoing and come near to remorse. But then they harden themselves, boost their pride, and say, 'I don't care.'

This was a terrible thing for Pharaoh to do. If only he had allowed himself to be influenced at this point he might have been spared the troubles ahead. But having hardened his heart once, his pride dictated that he must do the same again.

Warn the children never to resist God's message, especially when it first dawns upon them. Whenever God touches their consciences and moves them with His love, warn them never to treat it lightly, or to shrug away such influences on their hearts.

(2) The frogs (*Exodus 8.1-15*). Describe how Pharaoh was next subjected to an invasion of frogs, which were symbols of life and fertility to the Egyptians. Normally they were glad to see frogs, for their presence meant that there was plenty of water nearby. But this time there were so many that they were horrible pests which made life unbearable, and even Pharaoh had to bury his pride and ask Moses to remove this plague. However, his change of mind was short-lived, for as soon as the frogs were gone he broke his promise to let the Israelites go.

Warn the children against breaking promises made to God. Perhaps they are touched momentarily by God's Word, but as soon as the feeling passes away they return to their old ways. Pharaoh lived to regret this.

(3) The gnats or lice (*Exodus 8.16-19*). Next God sent the plague of gnats or lice, things particularly detested by the Egyptians. Pharaoh's magicians told him — *This is the finger of God* — but Pharaoh would not listen to them.

Explain to the children that even the hard knocks, disappointments, illnesses and tragedies of life are allowed by God with a good intention — to bring us back to Him. They are designed to teach us that a life of rebellion away from God is hard and bitter. Urge your class to respond like the prodigal son who, when famine and squalor shattered his life of pleasure, *came to his senses* and began the journey back to his father.

(4) The insects or flies *(Exodus 8.20-32)*. In case Pharaoh was tempted to think that these plagues were natural events, God began to show him beyond all doubt that they were sent by the Lord. This next plague of flies only affected the Egyptians. The land of Goshen where the Hebrews lived was completely clear of these creatures. Egyptian flies gave rise to disease, especially serious eye diseases and blindness, so this plague would have terrified the people.

Pharaoh tried to compromise. He suggested that the Hebrews hold their feast, but within the land of Egypt. Moses would not accept this, and so Pharaoh promised again they could go, and even pathetically asked for their prayers (v 28). But once again, he went back on his word.

Warn the children against trying to bargain with the Lord. When He asks them to obey Him and live for Him, how easy it is to ease their consciences by giving Him a lesser thing. 'Why, I go to Sunday School once a week, what more does the Lord want?' Or, 'I will ask the Lord to make me a Christian, as long as I can hold on to some of my sins.' Pharaoh's compromise suggestion was only a way of keeping hold of what he wanted, and we should not fool ourselves either.

(5) The cattle disease *(Exodus 9.1-7)*. This time the animals of Egypt were struck down. Then — *the heart of Pharaoh was hardened* (v 7). By now Pharaoh was so firmly in the habit of resisting God, and of hardening his heart, that he was no longer a free man. His heart was made even harder by the Lord. The Bible here warns that this happens to those who deliberately and frequently refuse God's voice. Warn the children that if they constantly dismiss the Lord while they are young the day

may come when their hearts will never be 'moved' again.

(6) The boils *(Exodus 9.8-12)*. An even worse plague now afflicted the Egyptians — one which affected them personally. Plagues against the environment had not brought Pharaoh to his senses, so the plagues now turned against the health of the people. Sometimes the Lord shocks us out of living only for earthly pleasures by taking some of them away. But He may sometimes warn us by a serious accident or illness. Boils broke out all over their bodies. We read that the Lord hardened Pharaoh's heart. Was this cruel or unfair of God? No. He gave Moses the reason *(Exodus 9.15-17)*. It had been proved beyond all doubt that Pharaoh would not listen to God, however clearly God spoke to him. His doom was therefore certain. But God, out of love and mercy for us, chose to use Pharaoh as a warning to us that to resist Him is a horrible crime. Pharaoh himself was finished, but his sin is used by God to warn us.

(7) The hail *(Exodus 9.18-35)*. Let the children imagine the great thunderstorms which accompanied the hail. What a warning of judgement! The fifth plague (the cattle disease) had destroyed the meat, now the hail destroyed the barley. Step by step everything the Egyptians needed was being taken away. Now they were dependent upon meat and grain stored from previous years. As life goes by, the things which we depend upon for pleasure and happiness are often knocked away, yet men and women may still remain stubborn against God, as Pharaoh was.

(8) The locusts *(Exodus 10.1-20)*. Describe how clouds of locusts devastated large areas of the earth. Any crops left by the hail were destroyed by the locusts. The locusts left a scene of desolation. A once beautiful landscape, with all its prospects of fruit and grain harvests, was utterly destroyed. By now, Pharaoh's servants wanted him to relent. But when Pharaoh heard that Moses intended to take the Israelites, plus their flocks and herds (v 9), his greed got the better of him. The thought of losing not only his slaves but their animals also, was more than he could bear. Like a man who rushes back into a burning house to rescue his bag of gold, only to lose his life, Pharaoh had become irrational. This is why we warn against living for the things of this world and for possessions. In the end

they take us over and we cannot bear to lose them – even though it leads to our eternal banishment from God.

(9) **Darkness** *(Exodus 10.21-29)*. After three days of darkness in the land of Egypt, Pharaoh made his last offer, but it was still short of God's command. He sensed that this was his last opportunity, for he told Moses never to return. This time he threatened to kill Moses if he reappeared (v 28). How silly! Moses was God's messenger. Did Pharaoh not realise that the God Who sent the plagues could easily protect Moses? Yet desperate men curse God to their dying day – and it is a tragic sight. Show your concern that no child in your class will ever reach the point of just screaming out to God (in their hearts) – 'Go away! Leave me alone!'

Time had run out for Pharaoh. In the next lesson we shall see how the Lord had His way, His people being released without any loss to their lives. Loaded with Egyptian gold and silver they left the land of Egypt at the command of the Egyptians themselves!

Visual Aid

Teachers should look at VA 3 (see pages 26-27) before preparing the lesson. It summarises the chief points of the lesson. Older groups will follow the words – younger classes will watch the pictures while the teacher explains the words.

Redeemed! (51)
The Passover

5/18/08

Exodus 11 – 12.42; 1 Peter 1.18-19

Aim: To show the children what redemption means, and then to teach them how much it cost the Lord to redeem His people.

Teachers' Introduction

Like other great Bible illustrations the theme of redemption has stood the test of time and still provides a graphic picture, easily understood and appreciated by children, of God's way of salvation. Teachers should also read *Leviticus 25.47-55* and *27.1-13*.

One warning should be given. Whilst the term 'blood' is rich in meaning to Christians, it must be remembered that this word

LESSONS FOR LIFE

has quite different associations for non-Christian children. Little children can be unnecessarily disturbed by a wrong emphasis of this word. We would be grieved if they went home imagining we were a strange cult which revered sacrifices of blood. So it is important that we ensure that we express ourselves clearly to young minds, and follow closely the biblical pattern.

Lesson Outline

Remind the class of the tragic state of the Hebrews, learned in previous lessons. Ask the children in what sense *we* could be said to be slaves. Explain that in those days individual slaves could be freed if others were willing to buy their freedom. This process was called *redemption*. Younger children could picture a young lad being sold as a slave when his family was too poor to keep him, but as soon as his older brother could save enough money he would approach the boy's slave-owner and arrange to *redeem* him. The older brother *redeemed* the younger with the power of money. God *redeems* by the power of His sovereign might and authority. (God did not actually pay Pharaoh for the Hebrews.) Redemption illustrates:–

(i) The weakness and helplessness of the slave or captive who cannot free himself.

(ii) The sense of kinship or love and mercy which motivates the one who redeems.

(iii) The result of the redemption – which is that the redeemer possesses the captive as his own, having paid dearly.

While the Lord paid nothing to Pharoah, the redemption picture is true of the deliverance of Israel in all three respects. God paid for Israel in terms of His concern for them, His exercise of power, and His patience and kindness towards them.

The mercy and power of redemption. Next, present the magnitude of the situation in Egypt. Who could possibly afford to redeem a whole nation of slaves? What slave-owner would allow his entire workforce to be bought out? Or what other mighty nations would go to war for *their* sake? Only Almighty God was able to obtain their release by His acts of great power and mercy.

Built into the event of redemption was a deep and wonderful

picture of the far greater price that God would one day pay to deliver people from the captivity of sin. Describe the events of Passover night, emphasising the following points:

(a) Moses instructed the people to take a lamb from the family flock. Remind the class that this was one of their very few possessions. They owned no property, no jewellery, no homes; just a few animals.

(b) The lamb was not to be a diseased, deformed animal, but a valuable young male without any spots or marks.

(c) They were to slaughter the animal and prepare it to be cooked, but its blood was to be kept and sprinkled on the doorposts of their homes. This was very important, for the blood would be a sign to the angel of death (who would visit Egypt that night) that the inhabitants belonged to God.

As soon as the blood had been brushed on to the door lintels, the family were to roast their lamb, hurriedly make some bread and prepare to move! This should intrigue the children. Go on to explain this mysterious course of events. Remind them that God had warned Pharaoh many times and Pharaoh had resisted the Lord. Now it was time for God to act.

That night God sent His angel to every home in Egypt to kill the eldest son in every family. The Egyptians (who for many years had drowned the young Hebrew babies) now felt the pain of death in their own families. From the palace down to the lowliest home every family was affected — except those humble homes of the Hebrew slaves which had the blood marks on the doorposts.

Urged to go! Imagine the result! The Egyptians, already weary of the plagues, now demanded that Pharaoh let the Hebrew people go. The Hebrews were amazed that after all Pharaoh's stubbornness, in one night the will of the tyrant had been finally broken without any battle or show of arms. The Hebrew first-born sons were grateful to the Lord for sparing their lives, and together with their families they gathered their belongings and hurried to leave the land, taking with them the valuables which the Egyptians were ready to give them at that moment.

The Lamb of God. So it was that approximately two million people (600,000 men, together with their wives and children) took their leave of Egypt, each family knowing that there was a sense in which it owed its freedom to the death of a *lamb*. God told His people that they must never forget that night. The Lord Jesus Christ spoke of it just before His own death. What does this great Passover night teach us? What does it show us about God's way of redeeming *us* from sin?

(1) Explain to the class that men and women are willingly under the power of Satan. They have chosen to turn their backs on God and preferred to obey the devil. However, their chosen taskmaster is cruel. He makes them serve him all their lives and then traps them in hell. Who can possibly free them from his grip? In addition, because of their many, many sins, people are deeply guilty, and condemned by God to be eternally banished. What would God have to do to secure the release of any of us from the guilt of sin and the bondage of Satan?

(2) Just as the Hebrews had to take one of their valued possessions — a lamb — so God had to give His only Son for us. Even before the world began, the Lord God was prepared to allow His Son, the Lord Jesus, to give His life for His people.

(3) The Hebrews had to take a perfect, unmarked lamb. When God paid for our release He had to offer Someone Who was without sin. Ask the class for the name of the only Person Who has ever lived without committing any sin at all. Explain that it was because the Lord Jesus had never sinned and therefore did not deserve to die, that He could offer His life to free us. He died instead of us, in our place. (Of course, God did not pay anything to Satan for our release. But the Saviour had to pay the price — the punishment — due to us for our sin, in order to rescue us from Satan.)

(4) The blood of each lamb had to be sprinkled on the Hebrew doorposts. Unless that lamb had been sacrificed, and its blood *trusted* for protection, the Hebrew first-born would have suffered like the Egyptians. They were *redeemed* with the blood of a lamb. This taught them that their redemption was far from easy. Life had to be sacrificed before they were free to go. It also taught that God's help was only given to those who trusted in it.

Not silver or gold. Show the class that it is not easy for God to forgive sin. We have wandered far from God, committed many grievous sins against Him and sold ourselves to Satan. Do we suppose that money could secure our release? If God were to offer silver and gold could we be freed? No, something far more valuable was required to redeem us — the most precious item in the universe. Jesus had to suffer the awful pain and punishment which rightly belongs to us, in order to set us free. As the apostle Peter said — *You were not redeemed with perishable things like silver or gold . . . but with precious blood, as of a lamb unblemished and spotless, the blood of Christ (1 Peter 1.18-19).* John the Baptist called Jesus — *the Lamb of God who takes away the sin of the world (John 1.29).*

Giving His only Son. Ask the class if they have ever really thought about the price which Jesus paid for the redemption of Christians. Have they ever realised that God, Who made all things, so loved His people and so desired their return to Him, that He was willing to watch His own dear Son die in agony on their behalf? Have they understood the words of the Lord Jesus when He said that He had come — *to give His life a ransom for many (Matthew 20.28)?* Have they ever thought about the love of Christ which caused Him to consciously take their punishment (if they believe in Him)? And have they grasped the need to trust in the sacrifice of the Lord Jesus for themselves?

If any Hebrew family had failed to take the protection of the sacrificed lamb and paint the blood on the doorposts of their house, they would not have been protected from the angel of death. It would not have helped them at all to believe or respect the instructions if they did not carry them out and place themselves under the protection of the blood of the sacrificed lamb. So today, we cannot have our sins forgiven by God, nor be given a new heart and life by God, nor have His blessing, nor go to Heaven, unless we put ourselves under the care and protection of the Lamb of God, the Saviour — which means that we must give our lives to Him, trust in Him, and ask Him to forgive and save us.

Visual Aid

Draw an old wooden door bordered by two doorposts and a stone lintel. As you explain what happened on Passover night, colour the doorposts and lintels red to indicate that these were daubed with the blood of the lamb. Beneath the picture you can write the words quoted from *1 Peter 1.18-19* and encourage the children to learn them.

Guidance (52)   5/25/08
The Israelites Set Out on Their Journey
Exodus 13.17-22

Aim: To show how pointless life is without God. To describe the Christian life as a great journey which is full of purpose, and directed by the Lord.

Teachers' Introduction

During the course of the next three lessons we shall not only speak of the amazing events which the Hebrews experienced, but we shall show that all Christians experience the guidance and intervention of the Lord in their lives. This will provide a Gospel challenge for unbelievers and pastoral counsel for young believers in our classes.

It is easy for children to gain the impression that Christians turn their backs on the pleasures of this world solely to secure some far distant bliss in Heaven. These three lessons will give us lively, down-to-earth examples of the constant flow of wonderful experiences which fill the earnest Christian's life.

Lesson Outline

The journey begins. Ask the class to remember how the people of the Hebrew nation had been set free from the tyranny of Egypt in a single night (and without the use of military force). Describe the night of the Passover as the Hebrew families set out from Egypt with their flocks and herds, belongings, and the valuable items given to them by the Egyptians.

There were over 600,000 men numbered *(Numbers 1.46)* — altogether at least two million people including women and children. Help the children to picture the vast encampment.

(1) A destination. The Israelites would never have left Egypt, nor would God have brought them out, if they had not had some destination to go to. For hundreds of years the Lord had promised to bring them into their own land, *a land flowing with milk and honey (Exodus 13.5)*, the land of Canaan. Use the suggested visual aid (VA 1, page 13) to portray the journey from Egypt to Canaan.

No destination. Remind the class that the most important

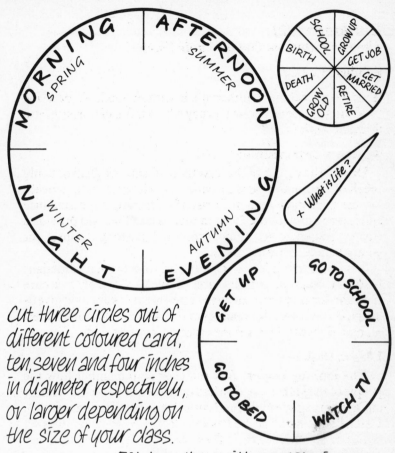

Cut three circles out of different coloured card, ten, seven and four inches in diameter respectively, or larger depending on the size of your class.

Fit together with a split pin, so that the 'what is life' arrow can freely rotate. Be careful not to obscure any wording when you make up the model. Rotate the arrow clockwise as you apply the lesson.

VA 4 — Visual Aid for use with Lesson 52 — 'Guidance'.

thing about any journey is the destination. Show the absurdity
of a family who set out for their holiday not having the vaguest
idea about which road to take, nor having any plans as to where
they are going. Compare them with the many people who set off
on the journey of life without any idea of where it is leading
them. They have little notion of what they want to achieve in
this world and they never give a thought to what will happen in
the next. Christians are different. They know where they are
going, and they see this life as a preparation for the wonderful
life which is to come, in Heaven.

(2) **A route.** The people of Israel left Egypt in haste. They
were not trained for such a journey. Only Moses had experience
of life outside Egypt, and there were many dangers and
difficulties ahead. Imagine the chaos caused if such a vast
company had been left alone to find their own way. Tell the
class of God's guidance. Describe the spectacular pillar − of
cloud by day and of fire lighting up the sky by night − which
God sent before them so that they would not get lost. Wherever
they were, at whatever time, they knew they must look for the
Lord's pillar of cloud or fire and follow it.

No route. There are many people on the journey of life who
have no guidance from God. Ask the children what life is like for
the typical worldling. It is all rather meaningless! Life's
experience can be summed up in the following way: −

> Morning, afternoon, evening, night.
> Get up, go to work/school, watch TV, go to bed.
> Grow up, get a job, get married, have a family, grow
>   old, fall ill, die.

Help the class to see from this how very little is gained from all
the struggle and worry which goes into life. When the under-
taker comes, it all seems to have been without point or reward.
Contrast this with the Christian life. The Christian's journey is
full of meaning and purpose. His life belongs to the Lord, to be
used by Him. God's Word guides him, shining out as a great
light in this dark world, giving clear and certain instructions.
Day by day, through all kinds of experiences, bitter or sweet, he
grows more like the King of the country to which he is going.
His desire is to live for the Lord in such a way that others

will want to join him on his great pilgrimage. Ask the class if they drift aimlessly through life. Urge them to give up the pointless drudgery of life without the Saviour.

(3) **At the crossroads** – **a guide.** Soon after leaving Egypt, the Israelites had a big decision to take. Which route should they follow? Should they take the direct coastal road, or should they take the longer but safer route through the wilderness? The Lord knew that to face the fierce warriors of the Philistines would demoralise the Hebrews, so He guided them southwards to Sinai – the longer route.

No guide. What happens to an unbeliever when he comes to the great 'crossroads' of life? Teachers could show a signpost pin-pointing the main junctions. Career – what job do I want? Marriage – will he or she make me happy? Home – where shall I live? Family – so many decisions! The unbeliever has to make all these decisions by himself. Occasionally he can turn to human counsellors, but they are likely to be just as fallible as himself. Christians have a wonderful Guide. Our Counsellor is none other than the Lord God Almighty Who knows all, sees all and is infinitely wise. More than that, He loves and cares for those who serve Him.

(4) **Under control.** The Israelites followed God's instructions, *And we know that God causes all things to work together for good to those who love God (Romans 8.28)*. Even hard experiences will be used by the Lord to our advantage.

Out of our control. Remind the class that a great deal of the unbeliever's life is outside his control. Most people talk of chance, fate or luck. Will the big decisions of life turn out well or badly? Will marriage go wrong, leading to misery? What will happen in life? The unbeliever has no friend in Heaven; no helper through all the events of life's journey. Ask your children if they want to rely on *chance* to shape the events of their lives.

How to join the heavenly road. Close the lesson by reminding the class that the way to God begins at the cross of Calvary. No one can join the road to Heaven without first seeing the need for forgiveness. We must repent of all the wrong in our lives and put our trust in the Saviour Who died in the place of all repentant sinners.

Explain that some people have hoped to get to Heaven by another way, eg: by following religious ritual. The Lord Jesus said this was impossible. He is the only Way; no one comes to God except by Him.

Visual Aid

The 'dials of life' pictured in VA 4 (see page 37) will fascinate the children and remind them vividly of the monotony of life lived without the Lord.

Protection (53)
Crossing the Red Sea   6/1/08
Exodus 14.5-31; Colossians 1.13

Aim: To give the children a graphic yet practical description of conversion. To help all seekers go to Christ in faith.

Lesson Outline

Remind the class of the amazing way in which the people of Israel, a nation of slaves, had been delivered from the land of Egypt on Passover night. Having been released from bondage they were now on the move. However, there was one great barrier to cross before they could leave Egyptian territory and celebrate complete freedom.

Some children will have experienced the novelty of passing from one country to another in times of peace, and enjoyed the excitement of watching passports being checked, treading on new soil, etc, and will be able to appreciate how much more significant such a step would seem to people escaping from enemy territory.

Explain that becoming a Christian can be compared to this experience. When any boy or girl is converted, that person leaves one world (Satan's kingdom of sin and darkness) and steps into another — the kingdom of God.

There may be some in the class who have had their eyes opened to realise that life in this world is a life of bondage; of slavery to sin. They have come to understand that it is possible to be set free. However, they may not yet have passed across the vital frontier.

Pharaoh's anger. Describe Pharaoh's rage as he awoke to the full realisation of what had happened. Help the class to imagine him thinking of all the half-finished cities now stripped of all their slave-hordes. He decided to go after his former slaves to get them back.

Danger! Tell the class how the Israelites reacted when they heard the thunder of Pharaoh's army catching up with them. They began to panic as they recognised their dangerous position. They were now trapped between the sea in front of them and the Egyptian army behind them.

People have the same experience when they first begin to seek the Lord. They cannot seem to pray very well; they cannot get on top of their sins; and they cannot really say they are converted. There still seems to be a great 'sea' between them and the certainty of knowing Christ. At the same time they feel that the sins of the old life are close behind them, ready to snatch them back at any moment.

What can be done? It was obvious that the Israelites could do nothing to save themselves. They had no weapons, they were weak, and they were cluttered up with all their baggage. They became desperate and complained to Moses.

Moses answered their cries with these words – *Do not fear! Stand by and see the salvation of the Lord (Exodus 14.13)*. This would be the key to their deliverance, and it is the key to our conversion also. Like them, we must recognise that we can do nothing to save ourselves. The barrier of guilt, like the roaring sea, lies between us and God, and we can do nothing to get through it. We cannot pay the debt of sin. We cannot make amends for our sin. We cannot overcome our sin. Neither can we escape from the sentence of condemnation which we are under. We cannot give ourselves spiritual life and power – which are essential parts of real conversion.

We need a rescue operation carried out by God. We must *stop* thinking that we can ever earn or deserve God's pardon. We must *stop* thinking that we can become Christians by any efforts we make. We must turn to the Lord, Who alone can save us.

Protected. That night the Israelites saw the great pillar of cloud, directed by the Lord, move between them and the Egyptians. Assure children that once they truly trust the Lord to forgive them and give them a new life, they will be ready to experience a miracle as great as the parting of the sea for the Israelites long ago.

Go forward! It was right and important for Moses to say to the people, 'Stand still!' But when Moses began to pray to God for help, God said, *Tell the sons of Israel to go forward* (v 15). Moses stretched out his hand over the sea and the waters parted, and the Israelites simply had to walk. God made a way for them to cross the swirling waters.

It is just the same when we are converted. Once we realise that we cannot save ourselves, and we trust solely in what Jesus has done on the cross of Calvary to take the punishment for our sins, and once we realise that we need God to change us, then we are ready to give our lives to Him and apply to Him for forgiveness. If we mean our prayer of repentance sincerely, and if we truly yield to Christ as Lord of our lives, then God (Who reads our innermost thoughts) will change our lives. We pray, knowing and believing that the Lord will hear us. We promise to give up our sin, certain that the Lord will enable us to do so. *Go forward!* says the Lord. We must apply to Christ immediately for the miracle of a new life.

A new land. Describe the joy with which the Israelites set foot on the farther shore. Picture them taking a breath of new air in another land. At last they were really away from Egypt.

Compare the experience with that of a new-born Christian. Suddenly the Lord has done for him what he could never have done for himself. He knows now that he has a new nature given to him, for he has no desire for his old ways. Instead of parting sadly from sinful ways – lying, tempers, cruel ways, and so on – he is glad to find that all these lose their power over him. He senses a whole new life opening up before him – a walk with the Lord through this world, leading to an everlasting life in the promised land of Heaven. Tell the children how conversion meant this to you.

The enemy defeated. The great Egyptian army moved forward with their warrior cries, and their spears and whips (so often used to beat the Israelites into subjection). Row after row of chariots set out to retrieve the slaves. The Israelites saw the dust, heard the terrifying roar of chariot wheels, the snorting of horses, and the shouts of a vast number of soldiers. But as they reached the middle of the sea, the Lord caused the Egyptian chariot wheels to break off, and they realised that He had done it, and panic set in. God commanded Moses, by a simple movement of the hand, to call the waters to return to their place, and the Egyptians were defeated and finished.

If we are converted, will Satan ruin everything and get us back to the old life? Will our Christianity last one week, or two? Will we want to return to our former ways? Will sinful habits have too much power over us? Not if we are really converted. Just as the pursuing army was defeated, so the old life is deprived of its power to take over once again. When we are genuinely converted, God keeps us right through life.

Urge your class to pray to the Lord to rescue and deliver them, so that they may enjoy the wonderful, almost indescribable joy of being *born again* from above. Suggest that any who have known something of this should share it with their Sunday School teacher. And any who are still 'trembling on the brink' can be assured that if they step forward in faith and real sincerity, they too will soon experience the power of God in their own lives.

Provision (54)
Food and Water Sent by the Lord

6/8/08

Exodus 15.22-27; 16.1-31; 17.1-7; John 6.26-35

Aim: To show that, far from being dreary and forlorn, the Christian life is full of adventure and many remarkable experiences. The miraculous provisions described in this lesson were used by the Lord Jesus as a picture of Himself and we must draw the same parallels.

Lesson Outline

(1) **Water at Marah** (*Exodus 15.23-26*). Ask the class to consider the problems which confronted Moses after they had left Egypt. Remember that there were around two million people to be provided for, and they were now in wilderness surroundings. Although parts of the desert (like Elim) provided some water and food, it was mainly devoid of supplies for such an enormous company. Describe the horror of the

Israelites when after three days journeying, they arrived at a large lake only to discover that the water was bitter and undrinkable. But they need not have complained to Moses, for before long they were to witness another act of God's power on their behalf. The Lord's instructions were simple. Moses only had to throw into the water the tree chosen by the Lord and the bitter water of this reservoir was made sweet and enjoyable to drink. What a remarkable experience!

(a) **Our thirst.** Explain that we have problems which can be compared to those of Moses and the Israelites. In journeying through the 'wilderness of life' we have great needs. Day by day we have a thirst for something better and more satisfying than this world can provide. Many children depend upon a diet of excitement and 'fun'. They depend on loud music and garish surroundings to see them through. But these 'props' can give no complete or lasting satisfaction to a human soul. Also, the entertainments and excitements provided by this world are, like the waters of Marah, polluted. Some of them are wholesome and good, but many of them pollute us, because they promote and encourage evil ideas, and are opposed to belief in God. These waters are bitter, because they influence our thinking and shape us as people.

(b) **Living water.** Describe the superior supplies which the Lord provides for His people. Jesus promised to give living water to all who asked Him (*John 4.10*). Explain to the children that He not only saves us, but He gives us a life full of meaning and purpose, and He is daily with us.

Suggest how believing young children can wake each morning knowing that the Lord of Heaven is watching them, and is with them. They can discover something new about Him day by day. Every time they come up against difficulties and problems they know that He, Who is almighty, is with them, able to protect and provide for them.

Far from being dull and monotonous, the Christian life is an exciting experience. Week by week the Lord helps His people in every area of life, including the struggle against sin and Satan. Often they can celebrate a victory, and even failure and disappointments drive them back to Jesus, Who is ready to go on forgiving when they are truly sorry. People who have been Christians for forty or fifty years or more will say that although they have often failed the Lord, He has never failed them. Many people look back on life with vain regrets, but not those who know the Lord.

(2) **Manna and quails** (*Exodus 16*). Soon the food which the Israelites had brought with them ran out and there seemed to be no way of feeding two million mouths. Instead of turning to the Lord, Who had so often helped them before, many of the people complained bitterly to Moses and wished they had never left Egypt.

But once again God was to demonstrate in an amazing way His kindness and His care, even to grumbling people. When the people awoke next morning they found the ground around them covered with enormous quantities of delightful, sweet manna. No bakers' vans were heard, but this bread from Heaven was delivered fresh every morning (except on the Sabbath) throughout all their journeyings. It could be cooked and baked (v 23), was small and flaky, was like white coriander seed (of the parsley family) and tasted like honeyed cakes. When they first saw it the astonished people asked, *What is it?* (v 15) Nobody knew, so they said — it is 'whatever?'! The word *manna* is the Hebrew for 'whatever?'.

In addition to this sweet food, the Lord sent a flock of quails at twilight to provide meat for the evening meal. No butcher organised consignments of poultry, but the entire camp was covered with birds sent by the Lord, and freely available for all. No history book records any similiar provision in the entire history of the world.

The manna which came down every morning from the skies to provide daily sustenance for the hungry Israelites was used by the Lord to illustrate how He provides spiritual and eternal life for all who believe in Him. Draw some parallels for your class: —

(a) **A free gift.** *It is My Father who gives you the true bread out of heaven* (*John 6.32*). Explain that just as the hungry Israelites found the manna outside their tents daily — a gift from Heaven — so the Lord Jesus and the eternal life He brings is God's free gift to us (*Romans 6.23*). Usually people had to plough the ground, sow the seed, water young plants, harvest the crops and mill the grain before they could have bread. The manna, however, just appeared — a gift which involved no sowing or labour on their part.

Similarly the Lord Jesus Christ gave Himself freely to us to be our Saviour. Only He could bear the punishment of our sin and purchase our forgiveness. Only He lived a life of perfection; a life good enough to earn Heaven for us. Salvation must be free. What 'work' can we sinners do to assist in our salvation? The answer is — none. Even our best efforts amount only to 'filthy rags' in the sight of a holy God Who knows our motives and searches our hearts. No human has ever lived a perfect life obeying all of God's commands. Even young children show how deeply anger, selfishness, greed and spite are ingrained in the human heart, disqualifying us all from Heaven.

Only the Lord Jesus Christ can make us fit for Heaven. He alone offered a life of perfect righteousness to His Father and it is only those who acknowledge their own failure and hopelessness, and trust wholly in Him and His free gift, who will ever receive eternal life.

(b) A life-giving gift. *I am the bread of life; he who comes to Me shall not hunger (John 6.35).* Remind the children of recent pictures we have seen of hungry people, with emaciated bodies, starving for lack of food. This is the kind of tragedy the people of Israel in the wilderness feared.

Can we imagine how hungry and weak our *souls* are without God's blessing? Do we realise we are like starving people, with no life in our *souls?* The manna gave life to people who faced starvation, and the Lord Jesus Christ brings *spiritual* life to all who believe in Him.

(c) Unfailing. The manna never failed. Not until they reached the promised land where it was no longer needed did their daily supplies run out, and that was some forty years later! Christian conversion means becoming a child of God — one who belongs to Christ Who never fails. It is not like joining a club or a new school. When someone is made a child of God, the blessing lasts for the whole of life, and then for ever. Also, Christians are always learning something new from God's Word, always receiving new experiences of the Lord's goodness — however long they live.

(d) For individual consumption. The Lord said to Moses, *I will rain bread from heaven for you . . . that I may test them, whether or not they will walk in My instruction (Exodus 16.4)*. Remind the class that the Israelites had to go out each morning and collect the prescribed amount of manna for their family (an omer per head) − *every man gathered as much as he should eat (Exodus 16.18)*.

The point reminds us that each one of us must come and believe on the Lord Jesus for ourselves in order to receive eternal life *(John 6.35 and 51)*. The Lord calls us one by one to follow Him. The tents of Israel were surrounded by manna but it was of no use to anyone who refused to collect and eat it. We may have Christian Sunday School teachers, a Christian family and Christian friends, but unless we believe in the Lord Jesus for ourselves, we shall never be converted *(Mark 16.16; John 3.18)*. Other people can pray for us, but only *we* can pray, 'Lord, forgive *me*, and convert *me*.'

Extra points. Older classes, already familiar with this narrative can explore verses 22-31 and learn lessons from the precise instructions given for the collection prior to the Sabbath, and the futility of breaking these rules. The terms of salvation are just as precise, and no other way will do.

(3) Water at Horeb *(Exodus 17.1-7)*. Moses was again in a seemingly impossible situation when the company moved on to Rephidim. They were deep in the wilderness now and surrounded by rocky terrain − the last place where they would expect to find water. Not surprisingly Moses turned to the only Helper he knew, and the Lord told him to strike a rock, from which water would come. Before long the people had ample water to drink and were reminded that they had sinned by doubting God's power. One day Moses would enjoy the great privilege of meeting God, and speaking to Him as it were, *face to face, just as a man speaks to his friend (Exodus 33.11)*, and the Lord would let Moses see His glory passing by *(33.18-19)*. No wonder God's people have often said that even the best things in an unbeliever's life are as refuse compared to knowing Christ and being found in Him *(Philippians 3.8-11)*.

Give some examples from Christian biography and church history of the way in which the Lord continues to bless and intervene in the affairs of life for those who labour for Him, and urge the children not to ignore such rich provisions while they are so freely available.

Series 8
Luke's Gospel (Part I)
PEOPLE WHO FOLLOWED JESUS

55 – A Young Couple
The angel had amazing news for this young woman of Nazareth. Are we as ready to listen and to act, when the Lord speaks to us?

56 – Working Men
These tough, hard-working men were not the kind to imagine the appearance of angels. What they heard and saw was no dream. At Sunday School we deal with real facts and important issues. Will God's Word lead us to the Saviour as it did the shepherds?

57 – An Army Officer
This centurion was an important and wealthy man, yet he humbled himself and realised how small and needy he was in the sight of God. Do we allow foolish pride to keep us away from God?

58 – A Housekeeper
Martha and Mary both had a lot to do, but when Jesus called, Mary gave Him first priority. Do we miss real life and Heaven for the sake of a hundred trivialities?

59 – A Wealthy Taxman
This man had made a fortune at the expense of others and so he was detested by the people and cut off by the religious

establishment. But Jesus had a mighty effect upon his life. No one is too bad or too sinful to seek His forgiveness.

60 – A Street Woman
This woman had been helped and forgiven by the Lord and wanted to show her gratitude. If we feel no gratitude or reverence for Him we can be sure that we have never really sought and found Him.

61 – Two Recruits
Following Christ is a serious matter which will change our entire lives. Jesus never made it sound easy. Instead of accepting everyone who volunteered, He showed them what conversion really involved.

62 – Children
Children have some very clear advantages over adults which help them to understand the Gospel. This lesson lists them. Do our children realise that they therefore have a special responsibility to hear and respond to the Saviour?

63 – A Sorrowing Widow
The Lord Jesus came to this woman in her hour of great need and did what no one else could do. In the same way He comes to give us the gift of life.

64 – A Dying Thief
This man had only a short time to live. No one thought he deserved to go to Heaven, but in these last moments the Lord Jesus performed such a miracle in his heart that he was assured of Paradise. Have you ever had such a conversion experience?

65 – Revision
Given certain key facts about the many and varied characters in this series, can we identify each one? More important, have we responded to the Saviour as so many of them did?

Teachers' Introduction to the Series
Children, like adults, often have their own mental image of a Christian. Some may imagine that only a certain kind of person (or even *class* of person) can be a Christian. Whatever their view or impression, this series will enable the teacher to show that the Lord Jesus called to Himself all kinds and classes of men and

women from all trades and walks of life. A glance down the list of characters featured in this series proves that the Saviour never limited His love and care to any particular group. This list provides a good cross-section of people represented in every day and age. Teachers can point out that this is a random collection from Luke's Gospel. In fact the Lord Jesus had even more types of person among His followers. We have not included, for example, Luke the physician, or the fishermen.

Our objectives therefore will be to convince the children:-

(a) *Whoever* believes will be saved — whatever their background, occupation, race, class, sex or country, or the period of history in which they live.

(b) Every Christian testimony of conversion is unique and special to that person. The Lord Jesus Christ calls each one of His followers in a personal and special way. We come to Him one by one, not as a crowd, or even as a family. Once truly converted, all Christians have their own personal testimony to His saving power.

(c) Nevertheless, the actual *means* of salvation is the same for every Christian. However widely our backgrounds differ, however unique our experience of the Lord, each must see himself as a needy sinner deserving God's condemnation. Each must put his trust in Christ alone and in His death for him on the cross of Calvary. It will be our privilege to trace this pattern in the case histories described in Luke's Gospel. We must pray that the Holy Spirit, Who has performed the operation of the new birth on so many in the past, will give us the joy of witnessing children brought to spiritual life through the means of these great examples.

Visual Aid

VA 5 (see page 51) is designed for use throughout the series. At the beginning of each lesson ask the class to list the characters they have already learned about. Then unfold the 'paper chain' to show whether or not they have remembered previous lessons. Teachers of older classes may want to print beneath each character the three points suggested in the revision lesson (65).

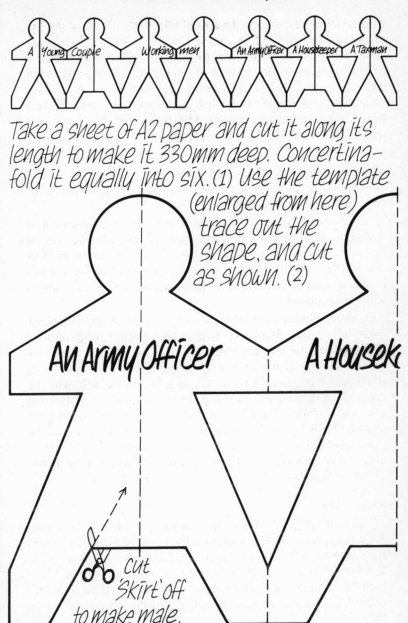

Take a sheet of A2 paper and cut it along its length to make it 330mm deep. Concertina-fold it equally into six. (1) Use the template (enlarged from here) trace out the shape, and cut as shown. (2)

An Army Officer   A Housek

cut 'Skirt' off to make male.

VA 5 — Visual Aid for use with lessons on 'People Who Followed Jesus'.

6/15/08

A Young Couple (55)
Mary and Joseph

Luke 1.26-38, 46-56; 2.1-7; see also Matthew 1.18-25

Aim: To show that the Lord God waits to receive and lift up those who come to see their sinfulness and their spiritual emptiness, and who put themselves in His hands.

Teachers' Introduction

At the beginning of this series we take the opportunity to present as a typical believer, chosen by the Lord, Mary the mother of Jesus. So often her experience is overshadowed by the events and excitement of Christmas and we overlook much of her individual testimony to God's grace.

Lesson Outline

Describe Mary, a young woman who loved her God and who was happily looking forward to her marriage to Joseph the carpenter. He, too, believed in the Lord and was ready to obey God's commands in his life.

Christian marriage – its benefits. Comment on the joy and true happiness which comes to all young couples who set out together on life's journey with respect for the Lord and His ways. Couples who scorn God's commands and go their own way may enjoy short-term pleasures but they miss all true blessing, help, and usefulness to God in their marriage. Sadly, also their union is often shallow and short-lived.

Help the class to picture Mary in her home at Nazareth, busy preparing herself for her wedding and the days which lay ahead. Point out – particularly to older classes – that nowhere in the Scriptures is she described as an 'especially holy person' or 'the greatest of all saints' to whom 'we especially pray'. (These phrases are quoted from a current publication – *The Teaching of the Catholic Church – A New Catechism of Christian Doctrine*.) On the contrary, before Mary had responded to his announcement, the angel called her *favoured*, for he said she had *found favour with God* (vv 28, 30). Ask the class to forget any previous ideas they may have had about Mary and turn with you to the Bible to learn what God's Word tells us about her. *Luke 1.27* describes her simply as *a virgin engaged to a man*. She recognised her need of forgiveness and called God — *my Saviour* (v 47).

A heavenly visitor. Describe the highly unusual angelic visitor to Nazareth. Imagine how Mary, a very ordinary girl, must have felt when the angel greeted her in such honoured terms. Mary could not imagine why the Lord's messenger should call her favoured and honoured among women. Point out to the class that in His Word the Lord calls all men, women and children to follow Him (the general call of God). Do we appreciate the honour of such a call? Do we think so highly of ourselves that a call from God can be dismissed without any serious thought, or treated as commonplace?

Mary was so different from most people. She was so honoured and surprised to hear the angel's words that she became very worried and afraid. The angel reassured her, saying, *Do not be afraid, Mary*, and went on to tell her facts almost too wonderful for her to take in. She was to have a Son Who would be called the Son of the Highest, Who would be given King David's throne, and Whose kingdom would last forever.

Describe Mary's concern for right. How could she have a son? She was not yet married. The angel went on to explain that the baby would have no earthly father but that God's Holy Spirit would bring about His conception, and He would be the Son of God. His birth would be brought about in an impossible way, humanly speaking, but possible to God.

Next, comment on Mary's reaction. There was no arguing, no doubting, no proud boasting — just humble submission to God's word. How much better it would be for us if we accepted the Lord's Word in this way. Instead we resist, we dispute, we reject all the gracious messages from God. True believers are those who receive His Word with trust and obedience like Mary.

A song. Without going into details of Elizabeth's experience, describe the occasion of Mary's song to the Lord (*Luke 1.46-55*), and note her humility and happiness. Read these verses with the class and help them to understand that Mary saw herself as being of *humble state*, a *bondslave*, and that she counted herself among the *hungry*, who needed to be *filled with . . . good things*. She rejoiced in the things which God did, not in the things man did. She looked at history and marvelled at the mighty acts of God for true believers. She took note of how God lifted them up, filled them with blessings and experiences of Himself, and helped them in all their affairs. The Lord still blesses those who acknowledge their need, admit their sinfulness and put their trust in His saving power.

God's choice. Suggest to the class that if they looked in the 'Situations Vacant' or 'Appointments' column of a newspaper, they would find that a person is only acceptable for a special post if *qualified*. This is the kind of person who is wanted in the world. But when the Lord God chose a person to give birth to His Son, He chose a humble young woman with nothing to boast about. She came from a very lowly town, Nazareth (a small country place, off the beaten track), and was engaged to a man who was no greater than a carpenter. God always likes to pass by the boastful, rich and mighty people, and to choose those who are sincere and humble towards Him. Remind the class that if they want to please the Lord they must turn their back on pride and pretended goodness. God hates those who put on airs and graces, and receives only those who approach Him humbly.

The promise kept. Briefly tell how an angel explained the situation to Joseph, and encouraged him to marry Mary and to take care of her and her Son, Who was the Son of God, the Saviour. Matthew's Gospel tells us how carefully Joseph followed the angel's instructions (*Matthew 1.24-25*). Describe how the couple had to travel to Bethlehem just as the baby was due. Explain why He had to be born in a stable. But though the world generally paid no attention to the baby of Bethlehem at that time, the words of the angel proved to be true. We shall hear more of this next week.

Encourage the class by showing that the same God Who chose Mary to be mother to His Son, our Saviour, still calls sinful men, women and children to become His children. And He still overlooks the proud and the self-righteous. While the Lord Jesus Christ was on earth He expressed a particular intention to call young children, looked down upon by adults, into His kingdom. Pass on the tender call of Jesus to your class and urge them to respond as Mary and Joseph did.

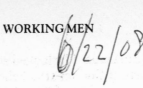

Working Men (56)
The Shepherds of Bethlehem

Luke 2.8-20

Aim: To show that some of the first men to find the Saviour in the New Testament record were far from being soft and naive types. To encourage the children to react in the same way as the shepherds did to the heavenly message.

Lesson Outline

This week we pass to another group of people — a group not so easily associated with religion. This lesson concerns tough and experienced working men. Talk to the class about these shepherds who were working a night shift and who had to be competent and fit to handle wild animals, cold temperatures, and raiding parties trying to steal their sheep. Describe also the quietness and darkness as the hustle and bustle of Bethlehem died down for the night.

Tell the class that the Lord God often deals with ordinary men, women and children in a sudden way. The world loves to make a great build-up to any of its special events, but the Lord frequently takes us by surprise. It could be a very ordinary Sunday when we set out for Sunday School, but unknown to us, God plans to meet us and speak to us.

A shock. Tell the class how even these hardy shepherds were gripped with fear as they heard an angel speaking. Explain that this is a normal reaction when people are first confronted with spiritual reality. When we first realise how great and holy God is, we also are humbled and alarmed.

For many years we may have lived far away from God, deliberately going our own way and trampling on His commands. Often we persuade ourselves that there is no God and that we have nothing to worry about. Then suddenly we come face to face with the possibility of meeting Him. It may be that we are challenged by a teacher or preacher who brings God's Word to us, or it may be that we are unexpectedly confronted with a very dangerous situation when death or disaster seem very close. Equally, it could be that we are looking at some wonder of nature when, suddenly, we know deep in our hearts that there is a God Who made all things including us.

The shepherds were especially frightened and awed because they *felt* the great glory and holiness of God shining about them when the angel appeared. They may even have thought that they would perish, and certainly they would have felt the ugliness of their guilty lives. Although we do not see angels today, the day we realise that God is truly there, and that we are sinful in His sight, will be a day when we feel alarmed and in need of God's kind mercy and help.

Good news of great joy. Describe how the shepherds' fear turned to amazed gladness as the angel delivered his wonderful message — that the Saviour, sent for all people, had just been born, as promised, in the city of David, the nearby Bethlehem. Read verses 10 and 11 slowly to the class and remind them that this was a message for the shepherds, and — still more wonderful — for us also.

For all who believe this message, it spells out the difference between a disastrous life and a meaningful one; eternal hell and eternal life. No better or greater announcement has ever been made. If the television newsreader were to announce that everyone was to be given a free holiday in an exotic tourist resort, it would be absolutely nothing in comparison to this announcement. Show the children that these words are the most important they will ever read.

An illustration. It is said that there was once a nobleman who had been condemned to die because he had spoken treasonous words against his king. As he lay in his death cell the night before his execution he had given up all hope of release or pardon. Unknown to him, a messenger raced on horseback to reach the prison before the dawn — the time for execution. The messenger carried a vital letter.

Half an hour before the execution the messenger arrived and the letter was placed with several others and delivered to the nobleman. He opened one letter (not the newly-arrived, urgent one) and found it was from an old enemy who wished him dead. In despair, he tossed all the letters aside and went to the scaffold to die. The nobleman was dead and buried when a lowly prison guard opened the rest of his letters. With a gasp, he found himself unfolding an impressive piece of vellum bearing the crest of the Lord Chief Justice. The letter, which was intended to be handed to the prison governor, ordered the release of the nobleman due to the king's pardon.

The words spoken by the angel to the shepherds were God's announcement that the Messiah had come, Who was the Way to eternal life. How many people will go to their graves without opening the most important 'letter' they could ever receive?

Praising God. Describe how the angel was joined by others, so that a whole host of angels celebrated this great occasion. Note that the proud, high-and-mighty ruler of Bethlehem did not hear any of this, but the poor, ordinary shepherds saw and heard it all. Any boy or girl who is proud and self-important will not hear God speaking, but those who stop and listen to God's message will hear wonderful and amazing things.

The reaction. Tell how the shepherds gladly left everything to hurry to find the new-born baby. We do not know whether they left anyone with the sheep. What did that matter on such a night! Now that they had seen and heard the angels, these men were convinced that nothing was as important as locating the Saviour. Every Christian has had this experience. Once they grasped that God had come into the world Himself to pay the price of their sin in their place, nothing else mattered! Apply this obvious point. Urge the class to set everything aside in order to find the Lord.

Not disappointed. Remind the children of disappointments which are so common in this world. A sale is announced, and the bargains are advertised as being spectacular. When we arrive at the shop, however, the few genuine offers have gone. But the shepherds found everything as the angels had told them (v 20).

God never breaks His promises. He never disappoints. The Saviour Who is described by your teachers is exactly as wonderful as they say. Mention some of His glorious acts and attitudes:—

(a) He came from the royal courts of Heaven to be born in a stable.

(b) He came to earth knowing that He must suffer and die.

(c) He came because He loved us and was willing to give His life to save us.

(d) He plans to take all His children to Heaven to reign with Him for ever.

Throughout the ages, anyone who has sincerely sought the Lord has found the experience of conversion to be just as real and amazing as Christians describe it. Urge your class to be like the shepherds and receive this great news with awe and wonder, so that they too will glorify and praise God for all the things He has done.

They made it known. Close the lesson by referring to verses 17 and 18. Right at the start of this Gospel we see that those who met the Saviour (even those who saw Him when He was a baby), felt compelled to share their good news with others. Urge your class to do the same. Even young children can witness for their Saviour.

An Army Officer (57)   6/29/08
The Centurion

Luke 7.1-10

Aim: To teach the children to look at the Lord in all His greatness, to feel their sin and unworthiness, and to believe that nothing is too hard for Him.

Lesson Outline
Teach the lesson under six clear headings: —
(1) The centurion's background
(2) His need
(3) His trust
(4) His shame
(5) His great faith
(6) Our faith

(1) **The centurion's background.** Today we learn about a man in quite a different class: a very well-educated man, trained in the Roman military academy and now serving as a high-ranking officer commanding a garrison in an occupied country. ('Centurion' was a term which had come to be used as a synonym for 'officer'. It did not only refer to a captain in charge of a hundred men, but to commanders of higher rank. The commander at Capernaum would have been at least a

lieutenant-colonel or brigadier in modern language.)

Describe life in the garrison at Capernaum, the Roman soldiers marching up and down in their breastplated uniforms to the sound of the orders of a 'drill-sergeant'. Like all soldiers they were being trained to obey orders instantly. On special days, the centurion in charge of the garrison would come to inspect them. His orders were given top priority. Explain that many officers were proud and haughty, interested only in their own promotion and success, and not caring much about the cost in terms of lives and suffering for their men.

This centurion was rather more friendly than most. He enjoyed a good relationship with the Jewish leaders and had even built a synagogue for them, which shows us that he was probably a high-born and very wealthy Roman. In particular, the centurion had a happy relationship with his personal attendant (nowadays in the British army called a batman), his slave, whom he valued as a very dear friend. For all his 'nice side', however, the centurion was no doubt very proud of being a well-born, well-educated Roman, and a successful commander, and all his confidence would have been placed in the power of money and the might of the Roman Empire.

(2) **His need.** Describe the day when his confidence was shattered. His slave fell sick, and soon it was obvious that his illness was very serious. No amount of commands to the medical staff could effect any change in his condition. Though the centurion was willing to pay the doctor's bills personally, no physician could help.

The centurion began to recognise that this was a situation over which he had no control. When it came to the big things of life, such as illness and grief, he discovered how small and helpless he was. Have we learned this lesson yet? Or do we imagine that because we live in the age of computers and modern drugs life can be successfully planned and organised to suit our every whim? Sometimes the Lord has to send tragic events into our lives to wake us up and make us realise how much we need Him.

(3) **His trust.** Describe how the Lord Jesus Christ had been teaching with great power in Capernaum and how He had done amazing miracles in healing the sick. The centurion must have heard of these events, and perhaps some of his men had mingled

among the crowds as the Lord had spoken. Just when it seemed that the situation was hopeless and the servant must die, the centurion became convinced that the Lord Jesus was God, and could help him.

Unlike the Jews (who were filled with all kinds of doubts and prejudices) the centurion was certain that if this Person could heal illness by a word of command, then He must be from God. Ask the class if they have ever come to understand that the Lord Jesus is Almighty God, with all power to bless seekers, or to judge those who ignore Him.

(4) His shame. As the centurion thought about this, he was overwhelmed by a sense of his own unworthiness. Who was he to be asking a favour of the Lord God? Other people might esteem him highly but the centurion realised that God knew his heart and all his secret sins. Could he now expect Jesus to help him?

Ask the class if they have ever felt like this. Explain that when people really think about meeting God, they begin to be overwhelmed by their unworthiness and sin. (Mention Peter's experience if there is time – *Luke 5.8.*) If we, like the centurion, want to ask God's help, first we must realise how great and holy He is, and how weak and sinful we are. (Perhaps we are proud of being a captain or prefect at school and we like other people to notice our achievements.) The centurion soon dismissed his success from his mind when the possibility of standing face to face with the Lord of Glory came home to him. How much more should we?

Explain that he felt so unworthy that he sent some of the Jewish elders to ask Jesus to heal his servant. They were very willing, and added their own tribute to the centurion's kindness and generosity. What an interesting situation this was! The elders thought that the centurion was a good man. But he himself was so aware of his inward sin that he dared not stand in the presence of the Lord! The Lord Jesus listened to the elders and soon set out for the centurion's house.

Describe the thoughts in the mind of the centurion as the Lord approached. He was relieved as he thought that his servant would soon be well, but suddenly he realised what he had arranged. The very Lord he was afraid to face was going to enter his house!

Why did the centurion feel like this? It was because he realised that *the Lord Jesus Christ was the Lord God*. Also, it was because he realised *Who God is*. The Lord God is awesome and holy. He hates sin, and He knows all about every single person. The Bible says *all things are open and laid bare to the eyes of Him (Hebrews 4.13)*. He can see into our hearts and He knows our most secret thoughts. All our horrible ways and thoughts are visible to Him. We cannot make excuses or lie to the Lord. He knows what we are really like.

(5) **His great faith.** When the Lord and the accompanying crowd had almost reached the centurion's house, a second delegation was seen coming towards them. What did they want? Surely Jesus was coming as fast as He could?

They had another message from the centurion for the Lord. He need not trouble to come any further. The centurion did not feel He could invite the Lord into his house. Instead Jesus need only say the word and the servant would be healed. The centurion believed Jesus could order illness about, just as easily as he ordered his own men (vv 7-8). Explain how the centurion would hear of some unrest at a distant outpost, and promptly despatch a band of soldiers to go and deal with it. He did not have to go personally. He dealt with problems by 'remote control'. He clearly realised that because Jesus was God, He could do the same. At a word He could heal from any distance.

The Lord Jesus Christ marvelled when He heard these words because they showed that the centurion had great faith. Alongside his sense of unworthiness and sinfulness, he believed with all his heart in the power of Christ (as God) to answer his prayer. Jesus turned to the crowd and preached a one-sentence sermon: *I say to you, not even in Israel have I found such great faith.*

(6) **Our faith.** What would the Lord say to us today? Do we have faith in Him? Do we, like those Jews, imagine we believe in Him, but really we do not, because we do not ask Him for salvation? Do we also, like the majority of those Jews, fail to understand our sinfulness? Do we really believe that the Lord Jesus Christ is Lord of all and is able to forgive and change us? Faith can be measured by our reaction to the Lord in real-life situations, not by whether we have attended Sunday School for a long time.

The result. By the time the messengers had returned to the centurion's house, his servant had been restored to full health. The Saviour never fails. If only we would trust Him as the centurion did, we too would see and experience great things.

A Housekeeper (58)
Mary, The Sister of Martha

7/6/08

Luke 10.38-42

Aim: To show that nothing in this world is so important as listening to the Lord Jesus Christ.

Lesson Outline

A personal Saviour. Remind the class that Jesus often spoke to vast crowds of people. On one occasion He preached to 5,000 men, together with the women and children who were with them. Many walked miles to hear Him. Sometimes such large numbers gathered at the lakeside to hear Him, that He would borrow a boat and speak from that to the crowd assembled on the shore. Yet in this lesson we find the Lord Jesus stopping at a simple home to speak to two sisters. Explain that although the Lord was great, He constantly found time to listen and speak to all kinds of ordinary people – unlike most famous politicians and pop stars today. *Lazarus / Brother*

Show the children a picture or model of an Eastern home, and speak of some of the differences between those homes and our own (eg: their flat roofs, fewer rooms, lack of modern facilities and gadgets). Mary and Martha were ordinary women who kept house. They were not powerful like the centurion, nor tough like the shepherds. Their routine was probably very drab and unexciting, and yet Jesus stopped to call on them.

Briefly apply this point by reminding the class that the Lord of Glory never overlooks them, whoever they are. Have they always thought that God is far away, and therefore not concerned about them? Do they realise that a real Christian knows the Lord and speaks to Him daily? Have they considered how offensive and sinful it is to ignore such a kind and personal God?

No time for Jesus. Remind the class of the hectic preparations which often have to be made when an unexpected

No home, 2 miles E of Jerusalem.
Bethany small

guest arrives at home. Describe how Jesus entered the sisters'
home. Mary took Him to the living-room and sat down to listen
to this honoured Guest. Now she had the opportunity to ask
questions and to hear answers which no other person could give
her. Tell the class of Martha's quite different reaction. She did
not seem to grasp the spiritual importance of the occasion. She
realised that what Jesus was saying was of interest, but she
thought there were more pressing problems to be attended to.

Suggest some of the chores which cried out for attention in
Martha's mind. Describe how *little things* became *big* to her. As
she fussed over every detail, so she became irritable, and began
to think that the situation was most unfair. She resented her
sister listening to the Lord, and before long burst into the room
with her complaints. The children will probably regard her as a
fussy person, but point out how like Martha we can all be.

We too can spend our time on things that do not really matter.
How many people say they are too busy cleaning their cars to
worship the Lord on Sunday? Many children rush off to a club,
and miss the opportunity to hear about salvation and Heaven.
How many adults give their whole lives to the *little things* or the
ordinary things of life, and miss the whole purpose of being here
— to seek and find the Lord? Explain that when we despise
God's Word and its teaching and give priority to other interests
and concerns, we sin against the Lord. Indeed, to snub the
Lord God is a worse sin than lying, stealing or killing.

Choosing the one important thing. Tell the class that the
Lord Jesus was not harsh with Martha, though she deserved it.
Remind them that despite the way we treat the Lord, He is very
gracious and understanding. He knows our weaknesses and if
only we would turn and seek Him we would be amazed at His
kindness. But the Lord never condones wrong, and He was
very firm with Martha. He told her that her sister had *chosen the
good part* and that He would not take it from her. Why does a
person listen to someone? Why did Mary sit listening to Jesus,
forgetting everything else? She listened because:-

(1) The subject excited her. Have you ever sat watching
television with such excitement that you would not allow
anyone to disturb you? Mary knew that the great experience of
conversion, which the Lord spoke about, was the most
interesting and exciting thing she could ever hear, so her

Continuing discussion — cross here

attention was riveted. *who for you?*

(2) The Speaker awed her. We always listen to those whom we admire as great people. Mary listened to Jesus because she realised Who He was. She was not entertaining the high priest (important as he was) or even the governor, Pontius Pilate. She was entertaining the Son of God Himself. How could she spare a moment for anything or anyone else while He was there?

(3) His information was vital and new. She knew that the Lord could tell her things which no one else could. Some children like to read magazines and encyclopedias in order to find out as much as they can. But the Person Whom she had the opportunity to question could tell her all the things which neither popular magazines nor encyclopedias explain — facts about Heaven and hell, about the future of this world and about the end of time, etc. The Lord knew all things. Above all, He knew precisely how He would arrange forgiveness and new life for those who trusted in Him.

(4) This conversation could change her for ever. We always pay special attention to announcements which really affect us. Remind the children that often they whisper and fidget at school, but when the teacher announces details of a special outing, silence suddenly falls. No one wants to miss hearing the arrangements, for fear of being left out.

The Lord was talking about matters so vital that if Mary had not listened, she might have missed the way to Heaven. He was now close to Jerusalem where He would be crucified, not for *His* sins, but for the sins of all the people who believe in Him. He may have told her that He would overcome the powers of death and sin and rise again on the third day. He may have told her how He would then ascend to Heaven, but she need not then be sad, for He would still hear the prayers of His people and watch over them from day to day. Probably He discussed with her how she could serve Him in this world, speaking to others of her Saviour. Then He may have spoken of the wonderful home in Heaven which He was going to prepare for her and all His people *(John 14.1-3)*, and how He would come to take her there one day.

We should listen also. Close by asking the class who they most resemble. Are they like Martha, too busy with other, lesser things to listen to the Lord; their minds too filled with sports and day-to-day excitements? Or are they like Mary, aware that the Bible is so full of vital subjects, and is worth their undivided attention? Urge them to seek the Lord Jesus urgently and they will soon respond like the Queen of Sheba when she met King Solomon and said: *I did not believe the reports, until I came and my eyes had seen it. And behold, the half was not told me (1 Kings 10.7).*

Lk 18:24 -27 Rich ruler

A Wealthy Taxman (59)
Zaccheus

7/13/08

Luke 19.1-10

Aim: To explain that the Lord Jesus Christ came to seek and to save the lost, and to urge the children to make a real response to the Saviour as Zaccheus did.

Lesson Outline

Tell the class the story of a *lost* boat; of how the rescue services are alerted and a search organised. Eventually the missing boat is *found* and its position is located. But this is not enough. The crew must not be left at the mercy of the winds and tides in their damaged ship. They must be *saved*, and so the rescue helicopter or lifeboat must bring the lost party to safety.

Use this brief illustration to fix the final verse of our lesson in the children's minds before the lesson itself begins. Explain that Jesus said that He had come to earth *to SEEK and to SAVE that which was LOST*. (Have these words printed on card.) Today's lesson will show what He meant.

(1) Lost. Many children picture Zaccheus simply as a pleasant little man whom Jesus called down from a tree 'for tea' (a misleading view which is fostered by one particular children's chorus about Zaccheus — a warning to teachers to look carefully at the words of songs before teaching them to the young). Set the record straight by following Luke's careful account:-

Rotten, corrupt, rich. Describe Zaccheus as the detestable man that he was. In order to make money for himself, he had 'done business' with the Roman occupying enemy of his country. He had bought the right to collect taxes from the people, and so he was able to extort and swindle his fellow countrymen as he wished. While he got richer and richer, many families suffered great poverty. Zaccheus had perfected this arrangement and was not just a local tax-collector but the chief tax-collector for that whole area. No wonder he was rich.

Help the children identify his type of person by suggesting some present-day examples of corruption and racketeering. Naturally Zaccheus was hated by the people, and would never have been seen in his local synagogue. While the Pharisees were religious hypocrites, Zaccheus was a completely *irreligious*, greedy, dishonest man.

As bad as the hypocrites. Possibly Zaccheus thought himself better than the Pharisees because he did not practise their hypocrisy. He may have regarded himself as being more honest because he kept away from the synagogue. Very often today people are put off Christianity by their bad impressions of the clergy, and they think they can live a better life by not going to church. However, the Saviour was so different from the Pharisees that Zaccheus listened very carefully to Him.

Needing a Saviour. The key point is that Zaccheus was lost to religion, lost to God, and lost to any kind of moral standard. Maybe the class think that only 'good', religious people can become Christians. Today's lesson teaches the opposite. Even those who appear to be good must confess they are lost and hopeless before they can be saved by the Lord. The Pharisees imagined they were good — but here we see they fell behind Zaccheus. The Bible teaches that — *There is none righteous, not even one . . . all have turned aside (Romans 3.10, 12).*

Curious. Zaccheus must have wanted to see Jesus badly. How do we know? *First*, because a highly unpopular man braved the scorn and hateful glares of the crowd. He ran ahead of the crowds to get a view of Jesus. *Secondly*, Zaccheus, though an irreligious man, risked making a fool of himself by being seen hurrying to hear a preacher. *Thirdly*, this proud, rich man appeared silly by having to clamber up a tree like a boy. He was determined to see Christ, even though he was short. Why should he run all these risks? Mere curiosity? Or was his rich life not satisfying? Was he really a very empty, unhappy man? Was

Same tall - opposite. -

he longing to find a meaning for life?

(2) **Christ came to seek Zaccheus.** From his undignified vantage point on the branch of a sycamore tree, Zaccheus watched as Jesus approached. All he wanted to do was watch. He would probably have liked to have been invisible or to have hidden in the tree so that he could listen unseen. What would Jesus do or say? Suddenly he received a terrible shock. Something happened which he could never have expected. Describe his surprise as the Saviour stopped beneath the tree, called him by name, told him to hurry and announced that He was coming to stay at his house. It was as though Jesus expected him to be up that tree, knew his name and his circumstances, and had gone to Jericho especially to find Zaccheus.

Christ seeks us. Apply these points:

We come to God sincerely only when we begin to realise how empty our lives are without the Lord. Suddenly, we develop a great desire to find out about Him. Then we do not mind what people say. They may sneer when we go to Sunday School, but that does not matter to us now. We want to learn about the Lord and about the way of salvation. After that, we feel the challenge of the Gospel to us. Like Zaccheus we discover that God is real, knows all about us, and is calling us in a personal way to come to Him.

(3) **Christ came to save Zaccheus.** The experience of Zaccheus shows us how thorough conversion is. God completely changes our ways when He converts us. As Zaccheus walked to his home the crowds jeered about his wickedness, and his own conscience troubled him. He felt miserable because of his sin.

Although his was one of the biggest, finest houses in Jericho, it was not fit for God's Son to enter. It had been acquired by dishonest means — by cheating and extorting money out of other people. Zaccheus knew that his achievements and his grand home must have looked foul in God's sight. He was probably amazed that Jesus should want anything to do with him. He was overcome with thankfulness that the Lord should risk His own reputation, and should have to listen to the criticisms being made about Him from the crowds along the wayside, all for the sake of an unscrupulous tax-collector.

Use this point to show that *we must feel the same*. We must realise that the Lord Jesus had to bear great pain and agony on the cross to save us. It was not easy for Him − even though He was the Son of God − to wash away our foul sins. It meant He had to go deliberately to Calvary in the face of all that hatred and suffer the punishment of all His people's sins, dying in their place. This was the only way by which we could be forgiven, and it should amaze us to realise that His love for lost sinners was so great that He willingly took it.

Zaccheus' response. Describe how Zaccheus stopped on the spot and *made his profession of faith* in the Lord. He did not wait until he reached the privacy of his house. He repented before the crowd, who would no doubt hear and demand that he kept his word. Before allowing the Lord into his house, Zaccheus confessed his guilt, admitted his unworthiness and announced practical measures to put matters straight. He would give away half his riches and restore four times the amounts he had defrauded. Of course, he surely repented to Jesus of all his other sins too.

Then something happened which was far more important than Jesus going into the home of Zaccheus. This was invisible to the crowd, but Jesus received Zaccheus into the 'household of faith'. A man who had been written off by everyone else had been *found and rescued by the Saviour*. Urge the class to be like Zaccheus, to make real and urgent efforts to seek the Lord. Any young person who sincerely prays and repents of his sin and earnestly wants to find the Lord, will be received by Christ.

Describe the board usually to be found at lifeboat stations bearing a list of the names and dates of all the boats and ships rescued. Jesus told Zaccheus that 'today' salvation had come to him. Ask the class if they can point to such a day, when their names were added to the list of all those whom Jesus came *to seek and to save*.

A Street Woman (60)
Who Washed Christ's Feet with her Tears

7/20/08

Luke 7.36-50

Aim: To demonstrate the attitude to the Lord of someone who has been saved, and to challenge the children by asking if this is how they feel towards the Saviour.

Lesson Outline

A bad woman. Describe this woman. Perhaps she was a friend of Zaccheus. She was immoral. She never went to the synagogue. She wanted money and did not mind how she got it. But as she grew older she became increasingly worried. Her good looks were fading and she no longer offered the same attraction to her clients. Most people looked down upon her, and people like the Pharisees would turn away from her in the street. She herself felt less and less happy. Doubtless she lay awake at night with a troubled conscience. And she probably had few real friends to offer her help or comfort.

No family support   culture

She finds the Saviour. Imagine her interest when one day she heard about the Lord Jesus, for He did not look at people like her with contempt. He was ready to speak about God to everyone, good and bad, rich and poor alike. He had changed the lives of people like Zaccheus and Matthew. He was more interested in saving lost people than in keeping the company of those who imagined they were already good. She listened carefully to Him and it is most probable that the Lord's preaching of those great words in *Matthew 11.28-30* were the means of her conversion.

Tears came into her eyes as she realised that He had come to save people like her. Jesus taught that God was like a father, looking out for his rebellious children to repent and come back to him. She went home and repented of her sinful life; not only of the terrible things she had done, but most important, of the fact that she had turned away from God and offended the One Who had created her. With shame and remorse she thought of all her sins. They seemed to her like a pile of dirt and filth, and yet the Lord Jesus Christ had indicated that He would take them all away.

She thought of herself as a poor, bankrupt wretch who could never pay her way to Heaven, and yet the Saviour had come to pay all her debts and give her spiritual life and riches which she had never dreamt could be hers.

Finding the Saviour ourselves. Explain to the class that this is what the Bible means by faith. It means that a guilty and lost sinner hears the voice of Jesus and believes what He says. Faith is not a strange, worked-up trust in something which is not believable. It is taking the real and living God at His Word; it is trusting what He says.

Ask the class:

(a) If they have ever seen their need to be forgiven their many sins — open and hidden, outward and also inward sins (such as pride, greed and selfishness).

(b) If they have ever believed the words of the Lord when He invites sinners to come to Him for forgiveness.

(c) If they have obeyed this call and repented of their sins.

The effect. Help the class imagine the extraordinary change which came about in this woman's life. Instead of waking up in the morning to grasp her tranquillizers or cigarettes (this is how it would be today!), she awoke with a real trust that the Lord Himself would help her. Instead of pouring out a drink to see her through, she turned her heart to God and prayed that He would be with her and help her to live for Him that day.

Meeting Jesus. Imagine her reaction when she heard that the Lord was going to visit a nearby house. Perhaps she could see Him! He might even speak to her! She knew that Simon the Pharisee, to whose house Jesus had been invited, would be disgusted if she entered his home, but she was determined to get in somehow. She took with her a jar of expensive ointment. She would take this for Jesus. It was costly but she wanted to express her love. Nothing was too good for Him.

Showing her love. Overcome with gratitude she burst into Simon's house and went up to the Lord, Who was reclining at the meal. She was so overcome that she cried, and when her tears fell on the Saviour's feet, she wiped them with her hair. Then she brought out her treasured ointment and applied it to His feet.

The Pharisees looked on with scorn and disgust, especially Simon who had decided Jesus could not possibly be a true prophet to allow such a woman to touch Him. But being a coward, he did not say anything. However, Jesus knew his thoughts. It is impossible to hide anything from Him. So He told Simon an intriguing story and then asked him a question. Describe the parable to the class. (Use banknotes to illustrate the point, if helpful.) Two people were seriously in debt to a money-lender. The first owed £500, the second owed £50. They could not find the money to pay, but he told them not to worry.

Help the class to picture the scene as the Lord asked Simon an apparently easy question: 'Which of the two would be most grateful?' The Pharisee gave his answer, possibly somewhat sullenly, suspecting a 'catch'. The Lord agreed that his answer was correct. The person who owed the larger sum would certainly be most grateful. But then the Lord immediately made Simon feel uncomfortable by drawing parallels.

The man who owed little. Simon was behaving like the second man. He did not seem to think he owed God much at all. He had shown none of the customary respect when Jesus arrived at his home, giving Him no water to wash. The woman, on the other hand, had shown tremendous gratitude and respect. This *proved* (v 47) that she had been forgiven her sin. (Verse 47 does not mean that she was forgiven *because* she showed respect, but the other way round. The fact that she loved much showed that she was a person who had received forgiveness, and a new life.) Simon the Pharisee had not received any forgiveness because he had never asked for it. Because he had never tasted or felt the power of the Lord, he felt no appreciation or love for Him. His behaviour showed that he thought he had no sin and needed little forgiveness. He thought he could earn his own way to Heaven without much help from God.

The Lord Jesus Christ did not go into the details of Simon's sins, such as pride, hypocrisy and jealousy. He simply pointed out that Simon should not be criticising someone else who had faced up to her sin and repented of it. He should not scorn this woman who, by expressing her gratitude, showed that she had received a blessing which Simon knew nothing about.

Who are you like? Ask the class into which category they fall. Are they like Simon, thinking they are good enough for God as they are? Or are they like the woman, feeling guilty and bankrupt before God, and in desperate need of His help here and in eternity? Are they overjoyed to hear that God has already made provision to pay the debt of their sin? The true convert is a person who has come to feel the burden of sin. Like a person in great debt, worried about being thrown on to the street, he is in great distress. Then the one to whom the money is owed freely forgives him! What relief and appreciation he feels. These are the feelings of a true Christian for the Lord God. How can we know whether or not we are really converted? By our love for the Saviour — our willingness to please Him and to give Him our lives.

Other notorious sinners. If time permits, remind the children of other people who were rescued by the Lord from lives of extreme and outward sin, such as John Newton. The ex-libertine and slave-trader subsequently devoted his life to Christ's service, and expressed his love to the Saviour in hymns we still sing. Warn the children that if they feel no love for the Saviour and no desire to please Him, then they are probably not truly converted, however religious their upbringing may be. Urge such to re-examine their hearts.

Two Recruits (61)
Who Were Shown the Right Way to Follow Jesus
Luke 9.57-60; see also Matthew 8.19-22

Aim: To show the children that if and when they follow the Lord, they must be prepared to part with everything else. To explain why this is so.

Lesson Outline   *7/28/08*

Explain that today's lesson is about two willing men who wanted to follow Christ but in the wrong spirit. Suggest that, having heard about so many people who followed the Lord, some of the class might seriously be considering doing so themselves. Children often move in groups. One craze follows another in the school playground. This lesson shows that it is possible to follow the Lord in the wrong way, and in today's lesson we see how He raised some obstacles in the way of those who approached Him wrongly.

A volunteer. Explain how the scribe came to Jesus making a confident promise: 'I will follow You wherever You go.' Yet the Saviour rebuffed him. Why? Contrast his attitude with that of Mary, the centurion, Zaccheus and the street woman.

They felt unworthy. Use this lesson as an opportunity to

Olympian

revise certain points from previous lessons. (a) The centurion did not even feel worthy that Jesus should come to his home. (b) He, and all the others also, felt their sinfulness and the need for repentance and forgiveness. (c) They believed that only the Lord could forgive their sin and help them. (d) They were amazed at His kindness, and were full of gratitude.

The scribe came confidently. (a) He showed no sign of feeling unworthy. (b) He seemed to feel up to the task, and expressed no doubts about himself or his ability to keep his promise.

Suggest he could have been like a certain enthusiastic young man who volunteered for the army at the outset of a war. He thought his country would greatly benefit from the addition of such a fit, strong, intelligent recruit, with such a good schooling and such leadership qualities. They would surely make him an officer. But when he came to have his medical it was discovered that he had a serious heart problem and he was sent home to his doctor who arranged immediate surgery. Instead of being a great asset to the army, as he had imagined, he turned out to be unfit! Instead of adding *to* his country's army, he really needed urgent help *from* his country's surgeons. Explain that no one is fit when they come to Christ. Before they can serve Him, He must take away their sin, cure their weaknesses, wash away their guilt, and forgive their debt.

The Lord tests the scribe. Just as the doctor took the pulse of the young army volunteer, so the Lord Jesus tested the spiritual health of the scribe. Instead of welcoming this professional man as a disciple, He gave him information which was calculated to turn him away *unless* he really felt a great need of the Lord's help.

Jesus explained that He and His followers had little enthusiasm for the wealth, comforts and achievements of this world. They belonged to a heavenly kingdom. Their home was in Heaven. The Lord Jesus Himself literally had no home on this earth. He had to forgo the most basic rights in order to do His great work in the lives of men and women. When God converts people to Himself, they have new aims, new delights and a new home. They lose their attachment to success and glory in this present world.

Some tests for us. In what spirit do we come to Christ? (a) Do we think that becoming a Christian is doing God a favour? (b) Do we imagine that bright, young people like us are just what He needs? (c) Do we come thinking that being a Christian will be like joining a super club which gives us advantages on earth and a promise of Heaven — like qualifying for possession of an international credit card which obtains special favours for its members wherever they travel?

Jesus tells us that when we come to Him we must come realising: (1) He must help us. We have nothing to give Him — only our poor, sinful, weak hearts which need His forgiveness. (2) We must be people who would rather lose everything in this world for the privilege of knowing the Lord Jesus Christ.

We do not know the scribe's reaction to the words of Jesus but we do know that countless millions of people down the ages have gone to Christ for salvation in the manner which He laid down, and none have ever regretted it.

The second willing man. Explain that other children may be more like this second man. He did not volunteer his services, but Jesus called him. There are many children who have heard their Sunday School teachers urging them to follow the Lord, and perhaps their response has been like that of the second man. The idea of following Jesus seems to have pleased him. But there were other things he wanted to do first, things which he thought just as important.

He wanted to bury his father. This may mean that his father was elderly and likely to die in the not-too-distant future. The son did not want to disrupt family life before his father's death. However, he also stood to gain an inheritance, and did not want to put this in jeopardy. In other words, he did not want to lose anything by following Christ. The Lord Jesus clearly knew there were other brothers and relatives who could nurse and care for his father, so He told the young man to follow Him straight away.

Our delay. Explain that many children make this mistake. They are interested in the Gospel, but first they want to do other things. Before they follow Jesus they want to (a) 'grow up', or (b) enjoy and achieve other things first, or (c) have some fun in this world, and engage in various sins and be like their friends for a while.

In other words, many would like to have a foot in both camps – to enjoy and achieve these worldly things and at the same time become Christians. But the Lord does not allow compromise. If we are to follow Him, we must put Him first. To delay following Jesus, even with a fine-sounding excuse such as this man had, is disastrous. Had he returned home, he would probably have stayed there. Warn the children against delay. Nothing is more important than seeking and finding the Lord.

Children (62)   *Aug 3 - 08*
Who Were Welcomed by the Saviour

Luke 18.15-17; see also Matthew 18.1-14

Aim: To prove to children that the best time to come to the Saviour is while they are still young, before they are overtaken by adult pride and cynicism.

Teachers' Introduction

Some teachers may, at first, be alarmed at the prospect of teaching this lesson which has very little narrative. In fact they should look forward to it with great anticipation because it has unique relevance to children. It begins with the occasion when children were brought to the Lord, and it demonstrates the special place they held in His heart.

In order to prove that children can be converted and walk with the Lord we will examine six key doctrines (expressed very simply) which the Bible teaches are essential for salvation, and show how each one is *particularly* easy to understand for children *because of their circumstances as children*! Indeed, each can in some measure be more readily appreciated and grasped by a child than an adult.

The idea of this lesson is to show children that they have a special opportunity to grasp the greatest and deepest message in the world.

Lesson Outline

Interest the children by showing them how different from almost everyone else the Lord Jesus Christ was in His view of children. Explain that most people look down on children and some even despise them. They push children to one side and consider them too young to understand anything important. The best adults tend to take only a patronising interest. Though we live in a day when societies boast that they fight for the rights of children to be fed and clothed and educated, we discover on investigation that the Lord viewed children in a way which was unique.

Describe how the disciples turned away the mothers who brought their babies and infants to see the Lord. They knew Jesus was fond of children, but they felt that these mothers ought to have realised that He had more important things to attend to.

Jesus rebuked them sharply for this attitude. He explained that, far from children having to grow into adults before they could come to Him, it was adults who would have to become like little children! What revolutionary teaching! Does the class realise that the Saviour takes children so seriously?

The Lord will never accept the excuse that anyone is too young to be His disciple, because He taught that it is easier for a child to grasp and obey the great truths which lead to salvation than it is for an adult (*Matthew 18.3*).

You may like to point out to the class that every really worthwhile privilege in this world — except becoming a Christian — is *only* available to adults. Only an adult may become prime minister or a pilot or a surgeon or a professor. (These privileges are open only to those who are adult, and who study or work for them for many years.) Only adults may vote or drive cars. But the Lord has made it possible for the greatest privilege of all — conversion — to be available to all, even to the youngest child.

Six essential beliefs

(1) **God created us.** Because He created us, He has the right to command that we should love and please Him. Ask the class — Is this too hard for a child to understand? Explain that adults are so prejudiced against God that they have invented all kinds of theories and philosophies by which they convince themselves that the world was formed without God. They welcome books and TV programmes which claim that everything came about by chance, human beings included.

Children, by contrast, have not yet been brainwashed by all this. If they look at the sky by day or night, or at the design of plants and animals, or think of their own lives, they instinctively know that God designed and made everything.

As children and young people their lives are lived under the authority and direction of their parents. They benefit from the security and care which their families give them. Therefore they above all people can appreciate the right of God, the heavenly Father, to rule His earthly children. They can easily see that He has a right to the obedience, love and respect of the people He has made, and to whom He gives so much. It is as children grow older and their hearts harden that they begin to resent God's claim upon their lives. Only then do they ask, 'What right has God to interfere?' Invite the children to acknowledge that they can easily grasp and accept that they are created, and owe their lives to their Creator.

(2) **We have sinned and must repent.** It is hard for adults to admit that they are wrong. Their pride tries to convince them that every judgement they make must be right. Children, by contrast, are constantly being told off for their failures. Life for many a child largely consists of being rebuked, grumbled at and criticised. Their constant questions show that they realise that they have much to learn. All this makes it relatively easy for them to accept that they are frequently in the wrong, and sinful.

In addition, most children have a very strong sense of justice and fair play. They are able to distinguish between minor misbehaviour and real faults, and are the first to complain if they are punished harshly for a minor offence, while a friend is let off lightly for a serious one. This proves that they can easily grasp how much they sin, and they are also able to understand that the sin of ignoring God is much worse than some other forms of bad behaviour. Children, therefore, have a greater readiness to acknowledge their sin than adults, who are often blind to their failings. Invite the children to acknowledge that it is easy for them to see that they need to repent, and press home their duty to act on what they see.

(3) **We must place our trust in the Lord to forgive us.** As people grow into adulthood they develop great pride and self-confidence. They do not want to think that they are hopeless, or that they have *no* merit or value in the sight of God. They resent the teaching that the only way to Heaven is through free forgiveness. Children, by contrast, are not given much of a

chance to develop such pride. Supposing a child breaks or loses a valuable possession. He may be sorry, but his small amount of pocket-money cannot replace it. He has no earning power of his own, and depends on adults to pay the cost for him.

This *dependence* of children gives them a great advantage over adults because it helps them to understand GRACE. It helps them to appreciate that though they may be truly sorry for sin they can never pay its price. Only the Lord Jesus Christ, by dying on Calvary's cross, could take away sin. Neither children nor adults have any hope of forgiveness except in Him – a damaging concept to adult pride but a readily accepted truth to children who not so long ago lay helpless on their mothers' knees, or who have brothers and sisters who still do. Invite the children to acknowledge how easy it is for them to accept that salvation must be given as a free gift, and press home their foolishness to refuse such a gift.

(4) We must be converted. Adults do not easily accept that they are incomplete people – with no *spiritual* life or understanding, and no contact with God. They are inclined to take pride in their experience of life, their education, their health and strength, their achievements, their jobs, their earnings and their abilities. They do not like to be told that they must become like children and be given by God a new start, a new heart, and a new character.

Children, by contrast, are used to the idea that they are not yet grown up. They know they will get much taller, and more knowledgeable, etc. Life is before them and they realise that someone who sees them now, and then not again for fifteen years, will probably not recognise them. Because they accept the need for 'growing up' they do not become angry or confused when the Bible tells them that they must be changed – converted – by the Spirit of God, in order to know God. That makes good sense to children and teenagers. They can easily see why it must be so. Invite the children to acknowledge that it is natural for them to see the need for them to change, and press them to include in this their *characters* as well as their *bodies*, and to seek the Lord's power.

(5) We must return the love of the Lord. Adults can be extremely ungrateful for the assistance or advantages they have in life. They quickly forget the good things people do for them, and can be very slow to show appreciation or affection. Often they are very mean and selective about expressing kindness and love, and they become very hard.

Children, by contrast, constantly return affection with affection. They naturally respond to kindness, and appreciate the person who clearly has a fondness for them. In the same way, once they truly grasp the love of Christ, and what He was ready to do for their salvation, there is a ready inclination in them to return that love. Invite the children to acknowledge that it is natural for them to return kindness, and press home the vital importance of responding to the love of Christ.

(6) We must take the highway to Heaven. How seriously adults take everything in this world — their homes, their jobs, their standing in the eyes of others! The older an unbeliever gets the more he clings to *this* world, and the tighter he shuts his eyes to the possibility of another. Children, by contrast, regard their present situation as temporary. Young children spend much time in 'play', and they realise this is not reality.

The real thing, for young people, is away in the future. Even in teenage, life is seen as only a training-ground. School subjects can seem very theoretical and frustrating. The *real* life is yet to come. All this makes it easy for young people to appreciate the Bible's teaching that the present life is only temporary, and that the *lasting* realm is to come. Even on this point, therefore, children have an advantage over adults, and it is not hard for them to see the great importance of yielding their lives to Christ in order to secure, by grace, a place in Heaven. Invite the children to acknowledge that they naturally expect *real* life to be in the future, and urge them to look beyond adulthood, to their everlasting future.

Conclusion. After spelling out to the children their 'advantages', move to a closing application by asking the question: When is it best, therefore, to seek the Lord and be converted — as adults or children? By now they should know the answer and give it readily. This will provide the opportunity for teachers to urge them to take the advice of (and believe the promise of) *Proverbs 8.17: Those who diligently seek me will find me.* How tragic it would be if they turned away from the Saviour at the time of life when they have the advantages of understanding described in this lesson. Remind earnest seekers that even in coming to Christ we are given His help. Just as the mothers carried and led those babies and young children to the Saviour, so the Holy Spirit will 'take our hands' as it were, work within our hearts and help us to come to Him, and to yield our lives to Him. Assure the youngest:

> *If I come to Jesus*
>   *He will hear my prayer;*
> *For He loves me dearly,*
>   *And my sins did bear.*
>
> *If I come to Jesus,*
>   *He will take my hand;*
> *He will kindly lead me*
>   *To a better land.*
>   (Fanny Crosby)

Urge them to pray:

> *Saviour, I will wait no longer,*
>   NOW *to Thee I come;*
> *And when life's short journey's over,*
>   *Take me home.*

A Sorrowing Widow (63)
Who Met the Lord of Life

Luke 7.11-16; Romans 6.23

Aim: To contrast the horror and pain of death with the joy and triumph of eternal life — a gift of God promised to all who believe in Jesus Christ, His Son.

Lesson Outline

It may be helpful to approach this lesson from an unusual angle. *Romans 6.23* provides such help for us and we can use its imagery to catch the children's attention from the start.

Refer to a wage packet (with some classes it may promote interest to produce one). Describe the pleasure someone may have at receiving their first one. Describe the horror we should register if instead of being filled with banknotes, the wage packet contained only a packet of rat-poison! To think that we had worked hard all the week only to receive a death wish. What fraud!

The wages of sin. Explain that people who serve sin are similarly tricked. Sin pays its servants or employees a wage, but the wage of sin is death. Men and women turn against the Lord and sell themselves to sin and Satan, and in the end this cruel master rewards them with death. Tell the children that the only Person Who can give us life is the Lord. He gives it to us as a gift, paid for at great cost to Himself at Calvary. Remind the class how He suffered on the cross for all the sins of His people; how He bore the pain which they deserved, so that He would have the right to pardon and forgive them, and to deliver them from death — the wages of sin. This incident, in which the Saviour restored physical life to a young man, teaches us about His power and willingness to give us spiritual and eternal life.

The sorrow of death. Describe the circumstances of this widow. Emphasise that widowhood in those days could be even more tragic than today. Wives were usually dependent upon their husbands. They could not easily become independent as they may do today. The widow of Nain would have continued to live in her little home, seldom getting outside the village where she lived. She probably had no income and depended on her son (her only son, remember) to provide for her and to give her any cause for joy and happiness. When in due course he got married, his children would be her grandchildren, and would light up her life. Describe the great blow his death would have been.

The power of death. Once death has struck nothing can be done. Even if the young man's mother had been very rich and able to hire the best doctors, once the young man was dead, that would have been the end. (The same is true today, irrespective of modern medical equipment. Once the moment of death is past, there is no hope of a person returning to life in this world.) Give some up-to-date examples of sudden tragic deaths known to the children.

Suggest to the class that it is easy to imagine that man with his many modern inventions and discoveries has everything under control. Remind them that there are vast areas over which he has no power, such as weather systems, and natural disasters

such as floods and earthquakes. The widow's friends and
relatives doubtless sent words of sympathy but not one of them
could bring back her son. She was left in her loneliness to follow
the funeral procession out of town to the burial ground. Urge
your class not to assume that life will follow the pattern they are
busy mapping out for themselves. Warn them of many unseen
dangers, and remind them of the ugliness and cruelty of death
however it strikes. A funeral makes people think of their
limitations. It is a warning to human rebellion against God. It
tells us that we cannot go on for ever behaving as though He
does not exist.

The gift of life. As the funeral procession approached the
gates of Nain, it encountered another procession — a large
crowd of people in a happy, optimistic mood. This crowd was
following the Lord Jesus Christ. Explain how the Saviour's
attention was moved away from those who followed Him, and
fastened on the tearful widow. Tell how typical this was, and
still is, of the Saviour. Even though seated in glory now, He still
notices and helps those who have need of Him.

First He spoke to the widow with words which were firm and
kind. Then He addressed the dead man with a strange command, *Young man, I say to you, arise!* Only the Lord Jesus, the
Prince of Life, could tell a dead body to get up and live again!

Remind the class that this was not happening in the middle of
the night in a dark room, but in broad daylight with two large
groups of people watching everything. Immediately the dead
son sat up and began to speak. No lengthy, delicate operation
was needed, as in a heart transplant today — just a few words
from the Saviour were enough. No faint pulse signalled the
gradual restoration of the corpse to life, but straight away he
could move and speak. Help the children to see that they have
every good reason to trust the invincible, life-giving power of
the Lord. This miracle was intended to show us His great power
not only to raise this dead son, but to give our dead *souls* life, and
also *eternal* life.

How can we begin a new life? Point out that we are not born
with this special *spiritual* life which we need before we can know
the Lord God. It must be given to us by the Lord, who called it
— being 'born again'. Just as the young man received his life
back again, and sat up, and saw the scenery around him, and

heard the excited voices of the people, so we *come to life* in a *spiritual* way when we are born again. God changes us, so that we *see* (understand about) Him, and read the Bible with new eyes. We *hear* the voice of God — not as sound — but we understand and respect His commands and His desires. We love Him, and 'get up' to serve Him. We have new feelings and joys. To be born again is in many ways like coming to life.

The instant effect. The moment the Lord gave the command, *'Arise!'* the young man lived again. And it is the same with being born again. When we ask the Lord to forgive us, and we sincerely trust Him and give our lives to Him, then He gives us new life instantly. Becoming a Christian is not a slow, difficult process, taking months or years. Whatever age we may be, when we seek the Lord with all our hearts, He hears us, and saves us at once. Many Christians know the exact date of their conversion; all can point to the particular period in their life when the Lord raised them to a new life with Him.

The Lord visits us. The crowd that looked on were filled with great awe and reverence when they saw what happened and said, *God has visited His people!* This amazing event showed them that Jesus was not just a carpenter's son from Nazareth as they had thought — He must be God come to visit His people with life and power.

Perhaps we make the same mistake as they did. We think of Jesus as a person in history and we have forgotten that He is God, risen from the dead, alive and real today, and that He really does meet with men, women and young people and touch and change their lives. Did you think that He never really comes near to people? But He does! And though He is Lord over all, yet He will visit us, no matter how bad, how dead in sin, however young or old we are, and give us new life if only we truly desire it. To be converted is to be *visited* by the living God, to be forgiven, and to feel His power changing us into real Christians.

Sin's wages or God's gift? Having outlined the way in which a child can seek the Saviour and His *gift* of new, spiritual life, urge them to go to the Lord admitting their sin and confessing that they deserve its *wages* — punishment and death. Show them they must be truly ashamed for ignoring the God Who made them, but assure them that because of His great love, He is willing to restore them just as He restored the young man of Nain.

A Dying Thief (64)
Who Was Saved at Calvary

Luke 23.32-43

Aim: To prove that the Lord can save the most hopeless cases, and to use the conversion of the dying thief to demonstrate the necessary steps in the conversion of any sinner.

Lesson Outline

Arouse the interest of the children by suggesting that this last person in our gallery of people helped by the Lord is perhaps the most surprising of all. There are two aspects of this conversion which will intrigue the children: (1) The thief was a dying man with only an hour or two to live. (2) He was a thief and an outcast. In all probability he was a violent thief, like those who in the parable of the Good Samaritan attacked people on the open road leaving them wounded and dying.

Remind the class that in those days there were no cars or vans to give security, and people travelling between cities with valuable possessions were very vulnerable to attack on the rough pathways which served as roads running through the mountains.

The two thieves crucified on either side of Christ had been caught and brought to justice. Describe the strange turn of events which meant that instead of these men dying a lonely, ignominious death outside the city wall, their crucifixion happened to fall on the same day as the crucifixion of a public and controversial figure. Great crowds were out to watch the death of Jesus of Nazareth, and the two miserable thieves found themselves in the midst of a great spectacle.

Describe the scene at Calvary, emphasising the following points: —

(1) The jeers and glee of the religious rulers as they gathered round the cross of Jesus. After all their plotting and scheming, their enemy was finally where they wanted Him. So often He had exposed their hypocrisy and sham. Now they had the

opportunity to get their own back. Jesus had claimed to be the Son of God, sent to save. Now, they thought, He could not even save Himself.

(2) Both the thieves were adding their insults (*Matthew 27.44*) to those of the religious rulers. Even in normal circumstances their language would not have been clean, but now that they were undergoing a very painful death, with the nails pulling at their flesh, and the knowledge that this time they could not escape, their curses were terrible. They were wicked men who had injured others. Now they faced death with a bad conscience. They cursed Christ because He represented righteousness. Possibly they hated Him for drawing large crowds who were watching their humiliating end.

(3) Jesus suffered most of all — because He was suffering not only the physical pain of the wounds received from the scourging and the hanging from the cruel nails — but something far, far worse. He was bearing the invisible punishment of all His people's sins. Above His head hung the inscription *King of the Jews*, and yet despite His cruel circumstances there was something majestic and divine about His Person. Instead of returning the curses of the rulers, He asked His Father to forgive them. Even in His great pain, He showed concern for His mother, and the repentant thief beside Him.

What changed one of the thieves? Explain that within a short space of time one thief changed from cursing Jesus to praying to Him; from reviling Him to witnessing for Him. How did this great change, this amazing conversion come about? Enumerate and clearly explain these several steps to the children:-

(1) **The thief heard a sermon!** The first part of the sermon was not spoken by anyone in words, but it was *seen* in the behaviour of the Lord Jesus Christ. The thief had never seen anyone like Him! Even though the Lord was nailed to the cross the thief could see in Him great majesty, holiness and kindness, and it dawned on him that Jesus was unique, and no ordinary man.

Then came the second part of the sermon, which was in words, but spoken by unbelievers! He began to hear the words of Jesus' enemies with new ears — *He saved others*. It was true the Lord Jesus Christ had given sight to the blind, raised the dead, and healed the sick! He had also transformed the lives of many people. How could this be explained?

Even as they continued to shout abuse, the thief found the answer. It lay in the insults of the Jewish leaders. (Without realising it, they were preaching a good sermon!) Some of them yelled out: *He said, 'I am the Son of God' (Matthew 27.43)*. They also challenged the Lord to save Himself: ' . . . *if this is the Christ of God, His Chosen One' (Luke 23.35)*.

(2) The thief began to ask himself − was it possible that Jesus was indeed the Christ, the King of the Jews? Although the thief was an outcast, he was still a Jew, and from childhood he would have known *Isaiah 53*, telling of how God's Righteous Servant would come to die in order to save His people. Was this man really the Messiah? It could explain His wonderful character (even when He was being so cruelly treated).

(3) The thief looked at the Saviour again. He remembered how He had been full of concern for others even while He was carrying the cross to Calvary. The thief looked again and saw the holiness and majesty of Christ, and His great mercy and kindness began to touch and melt the thief's hardened heart.

Suddenly the thief began to see it all. He and his accomplice were dying rightly, but the man between them had done no wrong. He *did* have the power to save Himself, but He was willingly dying in the place of sinners, being wounded for their sins. As the other thief called out another insult, this thief was no longer prepared to join in. Instead he took the side of the Saviour and rebuked the other criminal. The thief badly wanted to be forgiven, and even as he was dying, he wanted the Lord to take over his life. He wanted Jesus to be *his* Lord, and so he 'changed sides' and bravely defended the Lord Jesus against the jeering of his former friend in the hearing of the hostile crowd.

(4) The repentant thief prayed. As his life drained away this long-time criminal turned to the Lord, and the words of his first prayer tumbled from his lips. He did not know how to pray. He just said what was in his heart − a very plain and humble prayer − *Lord, remember me . . . (AV)*. What comfort and joy the dying man was given as he heard the precious words of Jesus, *Truly I say to you, today you shall be with Me in Paradise.*

(5) **The thief was saved** — in the very last moments of his sinful life. What amazing power the Lord Jesus had! Even as He died in apparent helplessness He gave this great demonstration of what He had come to do — transform the hearts of men and women, boys and girls. Even as He bore away our sin, He drew a lost soul to Himself. Remember what happened: the dying thief first grasped that Christ was the holy, sovereign God. Then he heard about His mission, that He had come to save sinners. Then he became deeply ashamed and sorry for his sin and showed this by 'siding' with the Saviour. And lastly he pleaded with Christ to help him — to save him. And the Lord heard.

How can we be changed? Ask the class if the Lord has ever changed them. What can we learn from the dying thief?

(1) We should look again very earnestly to the Lord Jesus. Anyone who looks at Him with unprejudiced eyes will see His majesty, His holiness and His great love in dying for sinners.

(2) We should believe what the Bible tells us about Him and His death. (Read such passages as *Isaiah 53* very thoughtfully.) The Lord Jesus was not a weak, helpless man. He was the Son of God, the Saviour, dying deliberately and willingly for all who would put their trust in Him.

(3) When we turn to the Lord our prayer, also, can be very short and simple, as long as it comes from the heart. Our prayer must be very humble as, trembling, we ask the Lord God to forgive and receive us.

(4) Like the dying thief, we must be ready to give ourselves to the Saviour and to take our stand for Him, whatever our friends may say, whatever others may think. And then we shall have the great joy of hearing His gracious reply and His wonderful promises.

> *The dying thief rejoiced to see*
> *That fountain in his day;*
> *And there may I, as vile as he,*
> *Wash all my sins away.*

Revision (65)

Aim: To test the children's knowledge of the facts and invite their response to them. To demonstrate again the wide range of characters who were converted to Christ in His day and to emphasise that He still calls all sorts and conditions of people to follow Him.

Teachers' Introduction

Two approaches are provided, which can be adapted for different age groups.

(1) **Who were they?** The first approach is a quiz of a 'whodunit?' kind. The clues are given in order of difficulty. Children should receive marks for guessing the identity of the person or persons. In the cases of those who are not named in the Bible, it will be necessary to tell the children that they are to guess their occupation or the identifying feature of their conduct. The sooner they guess, the higher should be their mark (eg: those who guess (a) receive 3 marks, those who guess (b) receive 2 marks, those who guess (c) receive 1 mark). This approach will provide a lively, factual revision for the series.

(2) **Have you?** The second approach challenges the children's spiritual position and further summarises the main points of the whole series. It consists of three 'applications' following each set of questions. Teachers should ideally use the suggested visual aid for this lesson.

A young couple – Mary and Joseph

Who were they?
(a) They lived in Nazareth.
(b) They planned to get married.
(c) An angel visited them both with very unusual news.

Application

(i) Mary realised she needed a Saviour.
(ii) Mary accepted God's will for her life.
(iii) Mary rejoiced and praised God for all He had done for her.
Do you?

Working men – the shepherds of Bethlehem

Who were they?
(a) Their job was dangerous.
(b) They received surprising news in the night.
(c) They found what they had been told about – in a stable.

Application

(i) They became aware of the great glory and holiness of God.
(ii) They listened to God's message with awe and reverence.
(iii) They acted on what they heard without delay.
Have you?

An army officer – the centurion
  Who was he?
(a) He was well trained for his responsible post.
(b) His servant was near to death.
(c) He asked Jesus not to come to his house.

Application

(i) He felt unworthy.
(ii) He believed Jesus was God, and needed only to say the word, to do great things in a life.
(iii) He believed in a manner which the Lord commended and blessed.
Do you?

A housekeeper – Mary, the sister of Martha
  Who was she?
(a) She lived with her sister.
(b) She put down her work for an important visitor.
(c) She was in trouble with her sister.

Application

(i) She put aside her earthly interests and put the Lord first.
(ii) She listened carefully to Him.
(iii) The Lord Jesus said that she had made the best decision.
Have you?

A wealthy taxman – Zaccheus
  Who was he?
(a) He lived in Jericho.
(b) He was very rich.
(c) He climbed a tree to see Jesus.

Application

(i) He was willing to risk embarrassment in order to listen to the Lord.
(ii) He was glad to receive the Lord's invitation.

(iii) He was ready to repent truly, by giving up his sinful gains. Are you?

A street woman − who washed Christ's feet with her tears
> Who was she?

(a) She was a notoriously, sinful person.
(b) She burst into a Pharisee's house without an invitation.
(c) She used her tears and her hair to wash someone's feet.

Application

(i) She was determined to meet the Lord.
(ii) She was overwhelmed by gratitude because the Lord had forgiven her.
(iii) She was willing to give a valuable possession to Him.
Are you?

Two recruits − who were shown the right way to follow Jesus
> Who were they?

(a) These men volunteered to follow the Lord.
(b) The Lord did not immediately accept them.
(c) They were made to take hard decisions.

Application

(i) They volunteered to follow the Lord without giving it much thought.
(ii) They tried to follow Him *and* at the same time remain 'on the world's side'.
(iii) They had to realise that following Christ involved turning from one pathway to another.
Do we?

Children − who were welcomed by the Saviour
> Who were they?

(a) Many of them were carried to Jesus.
(b) They were turned away by the disciples.
(c) The Lord blessed them.

Application

(i) Young people can easily understand they have a Creator.
(ii) Young people can easily see that they need forgiveness.
(iii) Young people can easily turn to Christ, and find Him.
Have you?

A sorrowing widow – who met the Lord of Life
    Who was she?
(a) She was with a large crowd of people when she met the Lord.
(b) The Lord was approaching her near a city gate.
(c) She had no husband or children left alive.

Application

(i) She had a problem which no person on earth could solve, except Christ.
(ii) She discovered that He had power to give life.
(iii) She, and all the people, realised that God had met with them.
Have you?

A dying thief – who was saved at Calvary
    Who was he?
(a) He was a criminal.
(b) He did not have long to live.
(c) He was promised a place in Heaven *today*.

Application

(i) At first he had no time for the Lord.
(ii) Then he realised that Jesus was God, especially from the things he heard.
(iii) More – he realised that the Lord was dying for *his* sins, and had the power to forgive him.
Have you?

Remind the class that you can mark their answers to the questions, but only they and the Lord can be sure of their answer to the application points. Show your concern for a sure and certain positive response.

Series 9
Exodus – Joshua (Part II)
The Christian Pilgrimage –
PICTURES OF SALVATION
AND HEAVEN

66 – The Golden Calf
The people of Israel, having pledged themselves to the Lord, engage in a drunken orgy around the golden calf, and God is angry. When we give ourselves entirely to the 'gods' of fun and pleasure, is God angry with us?

67 – The Day of Atonement
A brief glimpse into the ritual of the first Tabernacle – an illustration of the work of the Lord Jesus Christ for us.

68 – Refusing to Enter
The promised land is now close at hand. God promises His protection as the time to invade draws near, but suddenly the people are filled with alarm and fear, forgetting all that the Lord has already done for them. Do we also allow unbelief to rule – despite the evidence?

69 – The Brazen Serpent
The Lord Jesus used this as a picture of His death. We too can use this incident to urge our children to *look and live*.

70 – Jordan and Canaan
Moses and those who left Egypt are dead, but God keeps His

promise and leads Abraham's family to their promised land. May we also 'land safely on Canaan's side'!

71 – Revision of Series 7 and 9

An opportunity to retrace the journey from Egypt to Canaan in a swift overview, and to ask ourselves the question, 'Which point of the journey have I reached? Am I learning from the Lord on my spiritual pilgrimage?'

The Golden Calf (66)
Making Other Gods

Exodus 32

Aim: To compare the golden calf and the shameful orgy held around it with the modern gods of parties, fun and pleasure which seek to drag children down from a very early age in our society. To show that our dislike of these is not old-fashioned prejudice but well-informed concern.

Teachers' Introduction

Often we refer to worldliness and the gods of today in our lessons, but like the Word of God we need to be very clear and specific. Evil has become so open and widespread that many children step into its influence without being aware of its vileness or its consequences. Nor does evil affect unbelievers only. Believing children can become intimidated by others who scorn their lifestyle.

Lesson Outline

Ask the class to imagine how horrible it would be for a young husband to discover his bride in the arms of another lover only a few days after their marriage. Yet the people of Israel behaved exactly like this. Only days after they had solemnly promised to be God's people and keep His commands, they made an idol of gold, and worshipped it.

Bored. Describe how Moses had gone up to Mount Sinai to receive the ten commandments inscribed in stone by God Himself. No other people before or since have ever been granted such a privilege. Thousands of pounds are paid for great manuscripts bearing the handwriting of a famous author like Shakespeare. Crowds of people pore over such manuscripts in our museums. Imagine, therefore, the value of these stone tablets bearing words written, not by Moses, but by the Lord God Himself. More important were the laws themselves, designed by the Creator for the immediate and everlasting benefit of the people.

The Israelites waited for Moses to return from the mountain. He had not been gone for long when they began to get restless. Instead of thinking of the Lord and their past adventures they began to pine for fun and entertainment. They knew that the God of Moses would not condone sinful pleasure, so they went to Aaron asking him to make them other gods who would turn a blind eye to the wild party they planned. Explain to the children that sooner or later they will be tempted to ignore the Lord and the behaviour which pleases Him, and to give themselves to pleasing themselves in parties, discos, drinking, etc. Modern life is organised around many anti-God pastimes.

Why do we say that such activities are wrong and sinful? Is it because Sunday School teachers are old-fashioned? By observing what happened to the Israelites as they gathered around the golden calf and began their orgy of eating, drinking and having their so-called 'fun', we shall see how the *modern way* of getting pleasure is (in the same way) just as pathetic, insulting to God, degrading to human nature, and devastatingly harmful to our souls.

(1) **The cost.** In order to make the alternative idol, the Israelites had to bring some of their most valued possessions to Aaron. The treasures which they had brought out of Egypt had to be handed over, melted down and formed into the golden calf. Compare this state of affairs with ours. The gods of this world are costly. They demand heavy payment in terms of time and toil, and they frequently leave people stripped of their most valuable assets − their honesty, self-respect, chastity and loyalty. (Explain these terms briefly.)

(2) **The ugliness.** Describe the vile scene which surrounded the golden calf as the evening wore on. Imagine the noise of their drunken singing and dancing. Mothers − noted for their sensitivity, kindliness and beauty − lost all their dignity and threw themselves into crude and sordid antics. Responsible men, who had earned respect for their intelligence and

foresight, behaved more like animals, and became caught up in the hysteria of the moment.

The frenzied behaviour of that night was their way of turning their backs on the gifts God had given them as human beings. It was their way of saying, 'I don't want to be higher than the animals! I don't want to exercise *reason* and *self-control*. I don't want my *intelligence* or a *sensitive, affectionate* nature. I want to be free to do whatever animal instincts dictate.'

Explain how the gods of our world bring out the worst in us too. The thump of loud beat music drowns our sensitivities, and with the drink, the words of the songs and the style of dancing, people feel more and more willing to gratify their bodily desires without any self-control. These things work like drugs, and countless people are influenced by them and become dependent on them.

(3) **The sell-out.** Remind the class that at this stage of their journey the Israelites had everything to gain. Respect for them had grown in the surrounding nations. They could now move forward to take and enter the new land which the Lord had promised them. Yet this one night of frenzied sin threatened to end all their benefits. They were ready to sell their entire future for a few worthless hours.

This is the reason why Christians detest modern-day gods. Young people may be injured for a lifetime! The discos parade their boasted pleasures, but they do not tell us about the havoc which they create in countless lives. Discos, drug-parties, night clubs and pubs are the beginning of hundreds of thousands of forced and miserable partnerships and marriages, so often leading to violence and divorce, countless abortions and many other tragedies beside. Under their influence a life can be wrecked and ruined so easily.

(4) **The after-effects.** Help the class to visualise the scene the following morning: (a) the people felt sick and ill after their orgy of eating and drinking; and (b) they felt ashamed and pathetic as they awoke surrounded by the trappings of the previous night. Draw parallels for today. Many youngsters find their first escapade into sin a sickening experience – though they often try to hide this, and will not admit it. Their conscience aches though they try to suppress it.

(5) **Little gained.** Days later many Israelites probably looked back on that night and wondered what its attraction had been. Apart from the fact that it was over so quickly, was it really as great as they had hoped? Ask the class to imagine a child in a famine-stricken desert land who had found a rat's tail and was eating it. Supposing someone asked if he was enjoying it. Tragically, he might answer that it was the best thing he had tasted in months. How sad! How desperately hungry he must be to feel that way about such a vile thing. Today's so-called 'pleasures' are not much better. If only people could see that they seem attractive only if one has never known and experienced *real* happiness and excitement. Are we starved of real and lasting pleasures?

(6) **The selfishness.** Remind the children of all that the Lord God had done for the people of Israel. He had sent Moses, who was prepared to give up the rest of his life for their benefit. God had rescued them from Pharaoh by mighty acts of power, and He had prepared an entire land for them to possess. He had also painstakingly prepared His laws for their benefit. In return, all that they could think of was, 'We want our fun tonight. Forget about God! We don't care about Moses — he doesn't matter. What we want is a good time tonight!'

It is the same when we turn our backs on God's standards and, forgetting what we were created for, throw away everything for the sake of our so-called pleasure *now*. Children must ask themselves, 'Do I want to be a selfish person, thinking only of myself and *my* pleasure, and trampling over God's purpose in making me a special creature — a human being? Do I want to reject what Jesus did for me on Calvary in order to prepare everlasting life for me, just for this present, fleeting orgy?'

(7) **The consequences.** Describe how Moses was so angry when he saw the behaviour of the people that he took the two precious tablets — written by God's own hand — and smashed them to the ground. Why was he so angry? Why did he call it, *a great sin*? Why does God still judge this type of sin so heavily?

Explain that in doing these things people deliberately throw away their self-control and release their animal desires. They allow their 'lower' feelings to arise within them and stop at nothing to gain physical excitement and pleasure. When they do this, they are really saying something to their Creator. They are saying: 'I hate You for making me human – I'd rather be an animal. I was made in Your image to appreciate and enjoy high and holy things – but I do not care about that.' The instant people convey this attitude to God they deserve (more than ever) the sentence of everlasting hell. It is like voting against all that God has given them.

Close the lesson by reminding the class that in all our Sunday School lessons we chiefly emphasise the way to find God's mercy and grace. But it is equally vital for them to understand *why* God hates some of the pleasures which are fashionable today.

Our great need of a Saviour. This lesson may have helped children and young people to see the true nature and ugliness of sin. Show them, therefore, the great love of the Lord Jesus in coming to bear the punishment of our sin. As He hung on the cross, the Saviour, Who was altogether holy and pure, had to bear the pain of every impure, unclean act and thought, which *we* have indulged in. Encourage them to go to Him for forgiveness.

Younger classes. Teachers of young children will not want to go into such detail with the main part of the lesson, but they can effectively express, with horror, what happened around the golden calf, its ungrateful character, and the punishment which these events brought upon the Israelites.

The Day of Atonement (67)
A Meeting-Place with God

Leviticus 16; Hebrews 8 and 9

Aim: To teach seven simple but vital Gospel points pictured in the events of this great day.

Teachers' Introduction

This is a very fascinating subject and books could be written about the significance of the ritual of the Day of Atonement. Our task is to pin-point the great principles which picture (and make clear to the children) the importance and purpose of

Christ's work for us. Teachers should refer back to the last lesson in the *Mark* II series (*Lessons for Life*, Book 1, Lesson 17), *How Can We Go to Heaven?*, and Lesson 51 in this book on the Passover. They should observe the caution to avoid, (a) complicating the details of the ritual, and (b) wrongly emphasising the word 'blood'. In order to introduce a fresh aspect of the Lord's work for sinners, we shall emphasise His work as our High Priest in this lesson.

Lesson Outline

Introduction. At the same time as God gave the law to the people of Israel, He also gave details of the Tabernacle which they were to make. Like a doctor who diagnoses a serious disease and then prescribes an effective cure, so the Lord God, having identified sin in all its ugliness, laid down by a vivid picture the way of forgiveness.

At the feet of the golden calf the people had revealed how sinful their hearts really were. They were in no way fit to be God's children. As we consider the true state of our hearts we too must realise that we are unfit to approach the Lord. Something very great must happen to enable us to be reconciled to God. This is what today's lesson is about.

A map. All the children have seen maps. On a single page you can see London and Brighton and the roads that lie between. Of course London would not really fit on the page — nor would Brighton — but the map is a miniature representation which shows us all we need to know. The great 'act' which God had designed to bring about man's forgiveness would take place 1400 years after the time of Moses (when Jesus Christ came), and so God gave them a kind of picture or map to show how the Lord Jesus Christ would then deal with the guilt of sin. The picture could not itself save them, but it showed what God would do.

(1) A meeting-place. First, the people of Israel were to erect a meeting-place, a kind of church, for the Lord. As they were living in the wilderness and constantly moving camp, it had to be portable, and so it was called a Tabernacle, which means 'tent'. (Show pictures.) The existence of such a meeting-place taught them that God in His kindness was willing to meet with people and hear their prayers. Remind the class that God is not far away or unconcerned about us. He is a *Father*, and longs to restore the relationship which first existed between man and Himself before man sinned. He wants people to love and know Him.

(2) **The holy place** (Holy of Holies). At the same time God had to teach the people that it is not possible to enter into His presence unforgiven (as Aaron's sons had learned to their cost, *Leviticus 10.1-2*). Inside the first tabernacle or tent, was a second, hiding from view God's dwelling-place. A heavy curtain was draped around this area. No ordinary person was ever to enter this holy place, or they would die. This taught the Israelites that God is holy and that no sin or unforgiven sinner can live in His presence.

(3) **The curtain** (or veil). This was a constant reminder that their sin had put a barrier between them and God. The youngest child will know the feeling of having done or said something which puts an unhappy barrier between themselves and their parents. An apology or sorrow is necessary before things can return to normal. It is the same between us and God. Our sin must be dealt with before we can know Him and enjoy His blessing.

(4) **The high priest.** God made one exception to this rule. Once a year on the Day of Atonement, when the people kept a day of rest and repentance, the high priest was to enter the holy place to make an offering for the sins of himself and the people. This taught the people that one day God would send a great Mediator, or go-between, to represent sinners to God. Tell the children that the Lord Jesus is our Mediator or representative. Though God, He was born as a man and lived in our world being tempted just as we are, yet He never sinned. He alone was able to take our punishment for us, so that the Father could forgive our sins.

(5) **Sacrifices.** Before the high priest entered the holy place he was instructed to offer sacrifices of certain animals. As the people of Israel with their families watched the animals being killed and their blood taken as an offering, the seriousness of sin was impressed upon them in a very vivid way. Even the children were made to realise that their sin could not be forgiven without the shedding of blood, the sacrifice of a life. On this solemn

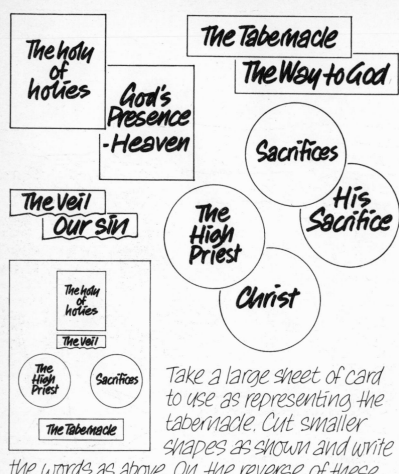

The holy of holies

The Tabernacle
The Way to God

God's Presence - Heaven

Sacrifices

The Veil
Our sin

The High Priest

His Sacrifice

Christ

The holy of holies

The Veil

The High Priest

Sacrifices

The Tabernacle

Take a large sheet of card to use as representing the tabernacle. Cut smaller shapes as shown and write the words as above. On the reverse of these shapes write the meaning of the various things that were part of the tabernacle in the wilderness. Use the drawing opposite to introduce the lesson, and the diagram above to explain what was in the tabernacle. Turn the shapes over to apply their meanings.

VA 6 – Visual Aid for use with Lesson 67 – 'The Day of Atonement'.

occasion they were shown a picture of God's way of forgiveness.

We know, as they knew, that the blood of animals cannot really take away sin. These old sacrifices taught them that one day a Saviour would offer His life for sinners. Only by dying for us could He secure our forgiveness. Whenever you hear or read about the animal sacrifices in the Old Testament, remember what they taught.

(6) A scapegoat. Describe the awesome gathering around the Tabernacle as the people waited for the high priest to emerge from the holy place to complete the next part of the ceremony. Show how two goats were picked for this day, one being offered with the various sacrifices (*Leviticus 16.5, 7-9*). However, the other goat was left alive for this next lesson. The high priest laid his hands upon the head of this goat and confessed all the sins of the nation. In a symbol or picture, this goat now seemed (though not really) to be carrying all their sins, and it was led out into the wilderness and set free, never to be seen again (vv 10, 20-22).

This was a picture of God's wonderful forgiveness. When we sincerely repent of our sins they are put on the Lord Jesus Christ, and punished in Him. He has already taken the punishment for all the sins which we confess to God in repentance. Once our sin is sincerely repented of, God will never remember it again. God removes our sins *as far as the east is from the west (Psalm 103.12)*. How seldom do earthly friends or relations truly forgive each other! Usually they still bear some grudge, and remember hurts and offences. But when the Lord forgives, He does so utterly and completely.

(7) A place of burning. The final part of the day's ceremonial was the carrying away of the bodies of the animals which had been slaughtered, to be burned at the place of the curse (see v 27; teachers may like to refer to *Leviticus 4.11-12*). Here, about four miles outside the camp, the sacrifices were turned to ashes. This taught the people that sin leads to a terrible punishment far away from the presence of the Lord.

If we die without ever having been forgiven, our souls must be 'outcasts', and we must bear the punishment ourselves. But if we sincerely turn to the Saviour and seek His forgiveness, we can be sure that He has already suffered our everlasting pain instead of us.

Conclusion. In closing the lesson make further mention of *a map*. People do not gaze at maps for pleasure, but in order to find where a certain place is situated, and how to get to it. The Tabernacle, with its sacrifices, was the Lord's 'map' of salvation (the 'way' to Heaven) given 1400 years before the coming of Christ. If we follow the map, and go to Christ for pardon and new life, we shall be saved.

Visual Aid

VA 6 (see pages 100-101) provides a picture of the Tabernacle in its wilderness setting which can be copied or enlarged, and also a diagram which will help point out the spiritual lessons.

Refusing to Enter (68) *Matthew 12:31*
The Result of Unbelief

Numbers 13 and 14; Deuteronomy 1.19-46; Hebrews 3.7-19

Aim: To warn our classes against hardening their hearts to the Gospel call by relating the bitter consequences of the Israelites' unbelief.

Teachers' Introduction

Hardening of the heart is a condition to be noticed and countered by all teachers. The book of *Hebrews* emphasises this lesson from the Exodus experience. After so many Gospel exhortations this theme will be particularly appropriate for our classes.

Many children consider offences such as murder, stealing and lying to be the worst sins, but the Bible places unbelief even above these for the destruction of the soul, and indeed, identifies unbelief as the root cause of other sins. It is one thing to disobey God's commands, but to ignore and reject the gracious invitation of our Maker altogether and to behave as though He did not exist, is the greatest insult possible to Him.

Lesson Outline

The promised land close by. Use a map to show that the people of Israel had moved from Sinai to the wilderness of Paran (*Numbers 12.16*). They were now only about 100 miles away from Canaan. Moses issued the instruction that they should now move into the land which God had promised to give them.

He anticipated their fear and reluctance to invade enemy territory, and assured them that with the Lord they need not be dismayed.

Reasons for trusting the Lord. Using this point as a means of revision, ask your class why it was *reasonable* for the Israelites to trust the Lord. Ask them to list the events we have already covered which demonstrated God's mighty power on their behalf. (1) The release from Egypt. (2) The opening of the Red Sea and Pharaoh's defeat. (3) The divine token of God's presence and guidance in the fiery, cloudy pillar. (4) The daily provision of enormous quantities of special food and water. (5) The demonstrations of God's hatred of sin seen in the punishment of those who turned to idolatry.

Pin-point each incident on the map. The Lord referred to ten occasions when He had proved His love towards them (*Numbers 14.22*). The whole purpose of God's leading them out of Egypt and providing for them in the wilderness was so that they should enter their promised land, but when the opportunity lay immediately in front of them, they hesitated.

Point out to the class that we may be guilty of the same sin. During this series in *Exodus* we have been at pains to speak about the wonders of the Christian life — freedom from sin and Satan, the daily enjoyment of God's love and provision for His people, the reality of knowing and walking with Him even in this life, and the promise of Heaven. Yet how many children turn immediately and without hesitation to the Lord? When we ask (like Moses), 'Who is on the Lord's side?' how many respond without reserve or delay? Describe how many of us find it the hardest thing in the world to leave our trust in this life in order to believe and obey the Lord.

Real evidence. This doubt of God's Word is wrong, but God in His kindness allows for our foolishness and frailty. He allowed them to send spies into the land (see *Numbers 13.21-23*). Describe their mission and the reports with which they returned. There was no doubt that the land was *flowing with milk and honey*. The spies brought back great clusters of grapes, as well as figs and pomegranates, to prove its fertility. What an advance on the arid desert where they were now existing!

The only problem which confronted them was the

inhabitants of the land. Even so they had no real need to fear. There were 600,000 Israelite men, and by now they were travel-hardened, tough and well trained in working together. The inhabitants of Canaan were divided into numerous uncoordinated groups in small cities and settlements, well separated from each other. Certainly they did not bear any comparison with the highly trained and well equipped army of Pharaoh whose destruction by God was still remembered by the Israelites. Yet ten of the twelve spies gave frightening reports of the enemy, portraying them as 'giants'. They described their cities as strong and fortified (v 28). They demoralised and discouraged the people (vv 31-33). As we know, God was quite able to make city walls collapse like a pack of cards before His people, and the Israelites had every reason to understand and believe this.

Still full of doubt. Yet immediately on hearing these cowardly reports, the people threw themselves into an hysterical outburst of unbelief and wicked criticism of the Lord and His servants. They even went so far as to appoint leaders to take them back to Egypt! How like them we are! When we have so many reasons to believe in God and trust His Word, we allow the smallest doubt or accusation to bring our faith to an end, and we scurry back to our world of pleasing ourselves in this life, and ignoring God.

Imagine what this means to God. Help the children experience the grief and sorrow caused to the Lord by the ungrateful, spiteful attitude of the Israelites, and compare it with our unreasonable resistance to God's Holy Spirit. Could God have done any more to reassure His people that He loved them; that they were 'the apple of His eye'?

Having made our children critical of the Israelites' behaviour, help them see that theirs is no better. Could God do more for us than He has done? Does He not remind us daily of His power and existence in the creation we see around us? As a result of scientific exploration we can now see and understand forces and design never known to these ancient people, yet we choose to build up our prejudice against God rather than to increase our love and respect for Him. We also know that God's love is so unfathomable that He was willing to make the ultimate sacrifice and to offer His own dear Son on the cross, so

that we might have our sin washed away. Yet we ignore even
this mighty act, and think of God as though He were an enemy.
Make your class see that doubting the Lord is a most
unreasonable and ugly attitude.

The consequences of unbelief. Describe God's righteous
anger at the Israelites' attitude and His immediate response.
They rightly deserved to be left to the full consequences of their
stubborn unbelief. If they chose to question God's willingness
and power to keep His promises, then He had every right to
abandon them to their own devices and to watch their destruction in the desert by the forces from which He had protected
them up till then.

If we refuse God's grace, we too deserve nothing but to die
without God and without hope. If we prefer to live without Him
(even without acknowledging His existence), then we can
hardly complain if we have to face eternity without Him.

God's mercy. Describe how Moses pleaded with the Lord,
mentioning His abundant lovingkindness and mercy, and how
God changed the sentence. Only the generation who had left
Egypt and rejected the Lord in the full knowledge of all His
power would die in the wilderness. God would keep His
promises, as He always does, and lead the Israelites on to
Canaan – but it would be *another* generation of them. Explain
that God does judge whole generations who wilfully indulge in
unbelief; who harden their hearts against His most tender
entreaties. Suggest that the middle-aged generation in Britain
today seems to qualify as such, for it is a generation that has
most wilfully rejected and trampled underfoot the worship of
God, and all respect for His Truth and His authority. Urge the
class to reject the prevailing unbelief of the masses, and to prove
the Lord for themselves. God is always ready to pour out His
blessings on young hearts – however heathen and against God
their environment may be.

Bitter anguish. Describe the anguish which descended on
the Israelites when they began to recognise the foolishness of
their actions. Their hostility to the Lord continued as they
pitted their determination against His will. Having heard the
sentence of death, they determined to show they could do
without Him and launched an offensive against the Amalekites

and Canaanites without His help (and contrary to His sentence). The consequences were disastrous.

Show the children that there are times when it is too late to seek the Lord. It is no good imagining that we can live without God and then demand forgiveness on our deathbeds. It is not possible to get pardon from some ceremony or act performed by a priest as we die. It will be too late then. Now is the time to take God seriously; to search earnestly and find Him.

Joshua and Caleb. Describe the brave, unswerving faith of these two exceptional spies who were willing to stand firm for the Lord, even when the rest of the nation threatened to stone them. Notice how the Lord stood by them and revealed His glory to them. Encourage young believers, and urge your class to trust God however hard and difficult Satan tries to make it. Assure them of His nearness, His power, and His determination to take all who believe in Him to the promised land of Heaven.

Conclusion. Close the lesson by expressing your concern that any of the class should miss the joys of knowing the Lord in this life, and of experiencing the indescribable wonders of Heaven in the next, simply because they believe the scorn and doubts about God which are spread around these days. What a tragedy that so many Israelites missed seeing their promised land! Even sadder if our boys and girls missed the wonders of conversion because of unreasonable, sinful unbelief.

The Brazen Serpent (69)
How Can I Be Saved?

9/14/08.

Numbers 21.4-9; John 3.14-15

Aim: To use the Lord's own illustration to show exactly how we approach Him to seek conversion.

Teachers' Introduction

Often we are at pains to teach the children the great Gospel truths — the key facts of sin, repentance, trust and forgiveness through the mercy of the Lord. But if there are those in our class who are earnestly seeking, do they understand how they must close with the Lord? Could there be some who, like the young

C. H. Spurgeon, know the *doctrines* of the faith, *desire* forgiveness, and yet still cannot say that they have exercised faith in Christ?

Lesson Outline

Sinning again. Explain how once again the people of Israel found cause to murmur and complain against the Lord and Moses. After all that the Lord had done for them, they still floundered in despondency and unbelief. They rewarded Moses (who had given himself to their care and safety) by telling him they would be better off in Egypt.

Reinforce the last lesson by reminding the children that we are little better. Though the Lord God has given us the privilege of life and so many other benefits also, we wilfully sin against Him. Even when we hear that He is willing to forgive us, we turn away from His call, and choose our own pathway in life. Then, when unhappiness and suffering enter our lives, we blame God, as though it is His fault.

The result. Describe how, because of their unfaithfulness, God withdrew His hand of protection from the Israelites. For years they had been living in a sandy desert, the home of many deadly snakes and other dangers, and yet up till this point they had been protected by the Lord. Their ingratitude meant that they would now feel the pain of His protection being withdrawn. Soon many were writhing in agony as a result of being bitten by a 'plague' of snakes sent by the Lord. What were they to do?

Repentance. They knew that there was only One Who could save them – the Lord God – so they went to His servant Moses. Though they had insulted and hurt him, they believed that he would overlook that and represent them before the Lord. He then interceded on behalf of the people, confessing their sin and asking for mercy.

God's remedy. Explain how the Lord made a remedy for their sin. Moses was told to make a fiery brazen serpent (actually in bronze) and to set it on a long pole. By simply looking up to this serpent any person who had been bitten would be cured. The serpents were not immediately removed, but the Lord in His mercy sent a cure.

Help the children to imagine how an afflicted person felt. Suddenly he would feel the sharp bite of a serpent. Soon he would feel terribly ill, and realise with desperation and fear that a deadly venom was in his body. If he was struck with remorse and began to feel truly ashamed of himself because of his faithless, selfish, complaining ways, he would say to himself, 'I will listen to Moses the man of God, and believe in the remedy which God has given for my sin.' As the fever grew worse he would go to where he could see the serpent of brass lifted high on its pole, and would look at it. Then, suddenly, the pain and fever would leave his body. To look at the bronze serpent was evidence of believing God's remedy.

If, however, the dying man remained cynical, continued to complain against God, ignored Moses and his message, and failed to look up to the symbol of healing, he would die. If he trusted instead in some other medicine — perhaps a herb — then he would die. God's method of healing would only work if the people *looked up and trusted*. It was obvious that they had to trust God as they looked, because a metal symbol could have no power to heal. Would the people do this? Would they engage in this simple act of faith and trust the invisible God to heal them? Tell what happened.

How can we be saved? Ask the children — Did you know that God saves us from the guilt of our sin in a very similar way today? How can we be forgiven and saved from eternal death? How should we approach the Lord?

Like the people of Israel, we must be truly in earnest to secure this salvation. We must realise that sin is killing us (spoiling our present lives, and leading us to eternal death). We must realise also that we can do nothing to save ourselves. We must be really sorry for our sin, especially for the way we have treated the Lord — ignoring His love, breaking His commands and murmuring against Him. We must also believe that when God tells us that whoever believes in the Lord Jesus Christ will be saved, He means these words. Like the people of Israel we must look at Him suffering and dying on the cross of Calvary. We must think of how He took the awful punishment of our sin in our place. We must realise and accept that we can be forgiven only because the Lord Jesus Christ has paid the price of sin for us.

A 'look' represents the easiest thing we could possibly do.

The youngest person can do it. The oldest person can do it. The poorest person, the least educated person, and even the very sick person, can look. In other words, the act of believing God's promise to save, and trusting in Him, does not require any goodness or quality in the lost sinner. It does not require long study or hours of deep concentration or special effort. Believing is easy — as long as we want to be forgiven.

To look means that we repent of our sin; we are truly sorry for it. (The Israelite who was not sorry for his sin was determined not to look at the bronze serpent. He was too proud, too obstinate, too sullen and bitter. Easy though the cure was, he could not bring himself to look to God.)

To look is a way of saying, 'I depend entirely on the Lord God for a free pardon, and for the healing of my soul. I can bring no offering, because I am just a lost sinner. I cannot help in any way towards my salvation. I humbly look to the Lord Jesus Who was once nailed to a cross and lifted up to bear the punishment of sin for me. My Saviour has paid the price of all my punishment, and I trust Him and believe in Him.' When we look to Jesus on the cross dying for our sins and we believe that His suffering was the only way by which our sin could be removed and we want Him to be our Saviour, then we shall be saved.

How long must we look? Just long enough to *see*! Do you *see* your sinfulness? Do you *see* why it was that only the Lord could take away sin? Do you *see* the great love of Christ in doing this for you, and the great price He paid to save you? If you see the point, and you really trust Him, then your whole life will be changed. You will be turned from being selfish to being kind, from being proud to being humble, from hating God to loving Him with all your heart.

Look — by thinking of the cross of Calvary and seeing the Saviour's love — until you realise that the Lord Jesus is not some distant figure in history, but your dearest Friend and Saviour; your Master and Lord. Look until you gladly recognise that 'love so amazing, so divine, demands my soul, my life, my all', and you give yourself gladly and willingly to the Saviour Who has given Himself for you.

Close the lesson by telling the class that even when Christians grow old and near to death they can rejoice and be happy when they remember the day they were saved. They have no need to

fear seeing God on His judgement throne, for they are saved by
Christ.

> *Look to Jesus, weary one,*
> *Look and live! look and live!*
> *Look at what the Lord has done,*
> *Look and live!*
> *See Him lifted on the tree,*
> *Look and live! look and live!*
> *Hear Him say, 'Look unto Me!'*
> *Look and live!*
>
> *Look! the Lord is lifted high,*
> *Look to Him, He's ever nigh:*
> *Look and live! why will you die?*
>   *Look and live!*
>
> *Though unworthy, vile, unclean,*
> *Look and live! look and live!*
> *Look away from self and sin,*
> *Look and live!*
> *Long by Satan's power enslaved,*
> *Look and live! look and live!*
> *Look to Him, you shall be saved,*
> *Look and live!*
>
> *Though you've wandered far away,*
> *Look and live! look and live!*
> *Harden not your heart today,*
> *Look and live!*
> *'Tis your Father calls you home,*
> *Look and live! look and live!*
> *Whosoever will may come.*
> *Look and live!*

(A children's hymn written by Philip Bliss on the theme of
this lesson.)

Visual Aid

It is easy to draw a serpent or snake-like creature and fix it to a
stick which can be held up at the appropriate time in the lesson.
Younger children are fascinated and it helps them remember
the point.

9/21/08

Jordan and Canaan (70)
Home At Last!

Joshua 1.3 – 4

Aim: To assure the children that the Lord has prepared a home in Heaven for all those who know and trust Him, and to urge them to discard the short-lived treasures of this world.

Teachers' Introduction

This lesson is about Heaven. Having warned the class of the consequences of unbelief in our last lesson, we move forward to offer every encouragement to those who put their faith in Christ as Saviour. We have some wonderful, positive notes to strike which should make the things of this world sound dull and vain in comparison. A brief glance at some of the hymns which anticipate Heaven, with their vivid and glorious descriptions, will add vigour and inspiration to the lesson.

Lesson Outline

After forty years. Remind the class that the first generation of Israelites to arrive in Canaan (those who had witnessed amazing tokens of God's power and willingness to save them) perished in the wilderness because of their unbelief. Only Joshua and Caleb survived to lead the new generation across the River Jordan into the promised land. It must have seemed a very long time for them to wait, but although the Israelites had been unfaithful to the Lord, He was not unfaithful to the promises He had made, and so at last the day came for them to take possession of their new land.

Ask the class if they have learned the great lessons of this series. Have they recognised that this life is like a journey? Have they given thought to their eternal destiny? Have they seen the foolishness of living only for this world?

The step of faith. Describe the new spirit in the Israelite camp. The people were now ready and eager to take the Lord at His word, to follow Joshua's instructions and to move forward. Instead of multiplying every doubt and dismissing the possibility of divine help, they moved into position. Only the River Jordan now lay between them and Canaan, but there were no boats or bridges adequate for such a large company with all their animals and belongings.

Nevertheless, instead of hesitating and murmuring, the people moved out of their camps believing that the Lord would provide. Even though the water level of the Jordan, very high at the harvest season, showed no sign of diminishing, the priests stepped out assuming that the crossing would be possible.

As soon as the Lord saw their faith He stopped the flow of water. Describe this dramatic event. Soon the priests (carrying the ark) and the people were crossing the river on dry ground. This not only enabled them to reach their destination, but had a great effect on the inhabitants of the land, who realised that the Lord was with the Israelites, performing great miracles like those they had heard of in connection with their departure from Egypt. Tell the class how the Lord proves Himself to us today as we take the first step of faith and trust in Him. We are soon overwhelmed by His kindness and the awareness of His presence with us. Give personal examples if helpful.

A new way of life. The details of the conquest will be taken up in a later series, but for the present we can give a general survey of life in the promised land, comparing it with the believer's joy in Heaven. The following headings may be helpful.

(1) Over Jordan – and home! Describe how the Israelites soon folded up their tents for the last time and moved into more permanent homes. The Bible describes our bodies as earthly 'tents' for our souls. When we die will we have any eternal home to live in? Christians look forward to death, when they will discard their sinful, failing, physical existence and take up occupation in Heaven. For them, death is nothing more frightening than crossing the River Jordan and finding themselves in their promised land.

(2) Fruit to eat. Describe the delight of the people, especially, no doubt, the children, when new and delicious foods appeared. Once settled in their new land, they could enjoy grapes and other fruit unknown to them before. Plants which would not flourish in the desert, however painstakingly coaxed, now blossomed freely in their new land. Similarly there will be very many great joys and pleasures when we reach

Heaven. Our struggle to improve in character here on earth will be at an end. In Heaven these virtues will spring up naturally and without effort.

(3) **Their own land.** The Israelites had wandered in the desert for forty years with no land to call their own. They had been regarded with suspicion and hostility whenever they got near to inhabited territory, and had been labelled as foreigners and enemies. How wonderful it was to be 'at home'. Christians look forward to Heaven because it is the home prepared for them by their Saviour. Satan will be unable to trouble them there. They will be welcomed by the Lord Himself, the angels and all those other pilgrims who have previously journeyed to the 'Celestial City', and they will be forever secure.

(4) **A land 'flowing with milk and honey'.** After many years in a dry and rocky desert, the land of Canaan with its pleasant climate and varied scenery was a delight to the eye. Daily the children could explore new surroundings. In Heaven, Christians will find themselves in a place of such breath-taking beauty that earthly words will not be adequate to describe it. All suffering and pain will be absent, and God's children will be filled with amazing happiness and joy. They will find themselves transformed so that they are absolutely honest, unselfish, and free from all temper and pride. In Heaven, God's children will suddenly find that they understand all the things they never understood before.

They will receive new bodies – bodies which never get sick, and which are like that of the Lord Jesus after His resurrection. He could even pass through the doors which were closed against Him. These new bodies will be altogether different from earthly bodies because they are designed by God for all eternity. Yet God's children shall know and recognise one another because there will somehow be many similarities with each person's earthly appearance and personality.

(5) **The land of Abraham, Isaac and Jacob.** Picture parents showing the Israelite children the landmarks where their forefathers had met with God: Bethel, where Jacob had dreamed his famous dream; Mount Moriah, where Abraham had been willing to offer up Isaac; and the field where Abraham and Sarah were buried.

On entering Heaven we shall be welcomed by many who have entered Heaven before us. All the great names of the Bible and of church history will be there. And we shall be astonished to see the angels. Heaven is a place of such power and beauty that it is impossible to describe. Eternally we shall mingle with others and explore the handiwork of God. But best of all we shall all see and know the Saviour, and find ourselves overflowing with love and admiration.

What must it be like to die and to find, suddenly, that one's soul is being carried away into a new world — a new experience — and that one's heart is filled with love and joy and excitement more than we have ever known before! Remember that such an experience begins here in this life when we take the first step of faith, repent of our sins, and trust in Jesus Christ as Lord and Saviour.

Revision (71)
Revision of Lesson Series 7 and 9
Exodus — Joshua (Parts I and II)

Aim: To discover how effective, or not, our teaching has been throughout these series.

Teacher's Introduction

Teachers should read again the points made in the revision lesson at the end of the *Genesis* I series (*Lessons for Life*, Book 1, Lesson 11). These series will respond particularly well to questions based on the visual aid illustrating the Israelites' journey and relating it to the Christian pilgrimage. Suggestions for questions and comments as they might relate to each great event are given below. Teachers will need to adapt these to suit the age of their class.

(1) **Slavery.** Ask the children about the horrors of slavery at the time our narrative begins. Ask them what it must have been like to be a slave in the land of Egypt under a cruel Pharaoh. Remind them about the slavery of sin. Who is *our* cruel taskmaster? Emphasise that God took the initiative in delivering the Israelites by sending and protecting the baby Moses. Ask which baby was given the name which means, *He . . . will save His people from their sins?*

(2) **Moses' choice.** Show the children the visual aid which illustrates the choice Moses had to make when he was a young prince. Why did he choose to leave behind the treasures of Egypt and associate with the Lord's suffering people? Ask the children about the choices *they* have to make as they set out on the journey of life.

(3) **Resisting the Lord.** Ask how many warnings God gave to Pharaoh before the night of the Passover. Show the illustrations you used. Remind the children how dangerous it is for them to harden their hearts to the Lord's messengers.

(4) **Redeemed!** What was it that made the angel of death pass over (leave alone) the homes of the Israelites on the night he visited Egypt? Show how this event pictures the protection we have by the blood of Christ — the death of the Lord Jesus — *our* spotless Lamb of God.

(5) **Guidance.** Picture again the feeling of freedom enjoyed by the Israelites as they set out from Egypt, led on their journey by the fiery, cloudy pillar. Ask how God guides His children today.

(6) **Protection at the Red Sea and the brazen serpent.** Emphasise again that it is far more important to be converted than to know the answers to Bible competitions, however good that may be. Ask which two lessons especially showed us how we can be converted. Remind the class that on each occasion the Israelites had to acknowledge that *only* the Lord could save them: once on the border of the Red Sea and also as they lay dying of serpent bites. On the first occasion they had to show their trust in His power and love by moving forward into the waters, and on the second occasion by looking up at the bronze serpent. Explain briefly how conversion includes trusting and obeying the Lord.

(7) **Provision.** Ask how God provided for the physical needs of so large a company in the wilderness. The Lord Jesus told His disciples that His Father always provides for those who put His kingdom first in their lives.

(8) **The golden calf and the Day of Atonement.** If time, ask questions about the Israelites' treachery and ingratitude as they

made the golden calf. Making further use of the diagram and picture, revise the lessons of the Day of Atonement. (If time is short, it may be that these are the best two lessons to omit.)

(9) **Jordan and Canaan.** Although this subject is the one most recently taught, we could not complete an overview the series' applications without reference to the Christian's heavenly destination. Close by reminding the children how anxious you are that they should be certain of a place in our Saviour's glorious eternal kingdom, whenever the time comes for them to 'cross the river' of death.

Visual Aid

Re-use VA 1 (see page 13) as you revise these series. It gives an overview, and shows the parallels for us.

Series 10
Luke's Gospel (Part II)
GOSPEL APPEALS IN THE SAVIOUR'S PARABLES

72 – The Rich Fool
This successful businessman is so wealthy that he can retire early. But God calls him a fool. Could it be that the Lord will describe us as fools also?

73 – The Lost Coin
Whoever thought that the angels of Heaven would care so much about a sinner who repents? The Lord Jesus describes how lost sinners are found.

74 – The Lost Sheep
We can see how unprepared a sheep is to go wandering off alone, but can we see how ill-equipped we are to survive without a Saviour? We also learn how the Good Shepherd rescues those who have gone astray.

75 – The Lost Son
A young man takes his share of a fortune, moves as far away as he can, and proceeds to throw it away on evil living. Our sin is to be compared with this prodigal's. God's great love is seen in this father's.

76 – The Grand Banquet
Imagine a crowd of vagrants, orphans and cripples attending

the Lord Mayor's Banquet! Many refuse to attend the marriage feast of the Lamb of God, so the Lord invites needy sinners to His banquet.

77 – The Good Samaritan
There is a striking likeness between the Good Samaritan and the Saviour Who told this parable. In many ways we resemble the man so badly in need of help. Do we recognise the only Person Who can and will help us when we suffer the buffetings of life?

78 – The Rich Man and Lazarus
A beggar is nursed by one of God's greatest servants, and a rich man begs for help in the flames of hell. God uses His servants to warn the next generation.

79 – The Pharisee and the Publican
There will be many proud, religious people who will not get to Heaven. Their place will be taken by those who have nothing to plead but their trust in the Saviour's blood.

80 – The Pounds
Our world is in a state of rebellion against its Maker. But He will return as Judge. He will not despise the effort of the youngest believer but will reward it with greater opportunities in His service.

81 – The Barren Fig-Tree
A wealthy landowner is disappointed that his treasured fig-tree turns out to be fruitless. The gardener pleads to save it, but it cannot be spared from uprooting for long. What if *we* remain unproductive for God?

82 – Revision
An opportunity to discover how much the children have learned, remembered and applied from this series.

Teachers' Introduction to the Series
These parables of the Lord Jesus will never cease to enthral us. As we approach this series, we must take note of some general themes:-

(a) Many of the parables deal with the end of life, Heaven and hell, and a person's eternal destiny.

(b) All the parables show that God's judgements are the opposite of what people may imagine. The religious Pharisee is shown to be evil; the successful rich man goes to hell as a poor failure; the priestly Levite has no compassion for the wounded man, and so on. All these parables contain an element of surprise because the Lord Jesus casts aside our preconceived ideas and shows how He sees things. We must get these surprises across to the children. Our great aim will be to show God's ways as opposed to man's ways.

(c) These parables are full of feeling and tenderness. If Jesus had outlined the truths He wished to teach in a weighty tome of systematic theology, it is doubtful if we would be moved by them. Instead He allowed for the hardness of our hearts by telling them in a form capable of touching the hardest person (by the influence of God's Spirit).

There is however a warning to be made in connection with younger classes. Little children find it difficult to draw analogies. They confuse the story and its meaning. If we say the shepherd is a picture of the Lord Jesus, they are likely to think that Jesus' work was out in the hills caring for sheep!

It is best on the whole to avoid drawing step by step parallels which give a meaning to every item in the parable. Better to relate the parable, and then to tell the children quite separately the truths it illustrates. The parable has a great use in that, if told properly, it will arouse all the feelings and emotions which we want to stir when teaching the spiritual facts. A detailed example of this is given in the notes on the parable of the Prodigal Son. All teachers of classes below 8 years of age should read this lesson carefully before starting out on the series. Such teachers must not be over ambitious, but tell the parable and make only the key Gospel application. There is no need for the younger children to understand every application; we can leave these supplementary applications for future years. Teachers of older classes, on the other hand, should apply the parable stage-by-stage, a method which encourages the children's attention throughout and avoids a long application at the end of the lesson.

Preparation. One thing is certain – these lessons need more, not less, preparation than usual. It is very easy to assume that because the parable is a vivid story it will be easy to relate.

However, we shall achieve nothing if the children go home with a knowledge of the story, but without feeling the truths it is meant to illustrate. When we make the *message* our aim, then the whole matter becomes far more difficult, and requires careful thought and planning. If we are willing to prepare our lessons conscientiously there is no doubt that the Lord will use these parables as He has done so many times before to enlighten many children and to bring them to a personal knowledge of Himself.

The Rich Fool (72)

Luke 12.13-34

Aim: To shock the class into seeing that a person considered highly successful by this world, may be a fool in God's judgement.

Teachers' Introduction

This parable is perfect for our day and age, and will be particularly useful at the beginning of this series. Although two thousand years old, it perfectly caricatures modern man with his huge self-confidence and his indifference to God.

Who are the rich? We must be careful not to suggest that the rich are literally the wealthy and upper classes. We must help the children to realise that anyone who boasts that he can do perfectly well without God's help is like the rich fool. The person in the parable stands for those who are self-confident and who place all their trust in *earthly* provisions. In *these things* the rich fool tried to provide for himself. (In this day and age, he might even be living on state welfare!)

The children should enjoy this lesson. They love to hear about the downfall of this pompous fool. After they have felt scorn for his proud stupidity, we can then tenderly turn the searchlight in their direction and ask them how like him they are (the method of Nathan in *2 Samuel 12*). We can then point our class to the Saviour Who came to give riches to those who recognise their spiritual poverty.

Lesson Outline

Introduce the lesson by asking – Did you know that the Lord

Jesus called certain people fools? Today we might use the word 'idiot'. You may be surprised to hear how the man He described as a fool was someone who thought himself to be extremely clever and bright. He was the kind of man we often hear of today. He had been so successful that he did not need to work any longer. Is this not the position most people would like to be in – possessing so much money that they could enjoy one lifelong holiday?

The particular man of whom the Lord was speaking was a farmer. Describe his shrewd financial dealings and how he amassed his wealth and made careful provision for the future. Explain how he was clever enough not to market all his grain in the years when there had been a bumper harvest and grain was fetching only low prices. He stored grain so that he could earn a fortune by selling it in the years of poor harvest, when it would fetch a high price. (This is a practice we are familiar with and the children will enjoy discovering that it is not confined to the twentieth century.) The rich man settled back in his splendid home and congratulated himself for his good sense and superb handling of business and life.

The rich man's outlook on life. Let us think about how this man thought and lived.

(1) He organised everything for himself. He was not interested in doing God's will. He asked, *What shall I do?* and answered himself, *This is what I will do*. Note the word *I*. He was the captain of his life, and he did what he wanted in life, not what God wanted. Is not this the goal of many people today – to please themselves?

(2) He did not believe in God. He said, *I will say to my soul*. He thought that his soul was just his own well-being; his own personality. He did not realise that he had an immortal soul within him, which lives on after death either in Heaven or in hell.   STEWARDS

(3) He was a very greedy and selfish man. He thought everything he could get his hands on was his very own property. He speaks of *my barns . . . my grain . . . my goods*. He did not accept that God made all things and that He is the *real* owner. The Lord lets us enjoy the ownership of many things, but expects us to be grateful to Him. The rich farmer stole God's blessings, and refused to thank or acknowledge Him.

what makes a rich person a fool?

(4) He did not believe that God is a King of great power, Who knows the very day when He will call each person into His presence. He said to himself that he had everything he needed — *for many years to come*. He foolishly assumed that God had no power to intervene in his life and that he could have as long a life as he wanted.

(5) He had very low standards and tastes. Listen to him. He says: *take your ease, eat, drink and be merry*. All he wanted was to be lazy, to eat huge meals and to get tipsy. He wanted fun for himself. He did not want to think of anyone but himself.

Disaster. Ask the children if there was anything the man had forgotten. Describe what happened that night. Vividly paint the scene of his leaving behind on earth all the riches which he had taken so long to acquire. Now, at the moment which mattered most, he was caught with nothing to show for the Lord. He did not know Him and had never served Him. He had *nothing* to take into eternity. His entire life had been spent on himself, and he had nothing to show for it which would please God. Instead of impressing his friends and neighbours with his wealth, his death made him appear as a fool who had worked for something he could never enjoy. Perhaps at the last moment it dawned on him with horror that his worldly wealth (his farms and crops, etc) had been given to him by God, Whom he had dismissed from his life.

Not the only fool. There are many people in the world today like this man. They are so proud of the things they own, but they do not give a thought for God. If God were to call them to Himself tonight how would they look? Have they anything to show Him in return for His love and kindness?

There are many children too who think only about the things they can get in this world, such as bicycles, new clothes, expensive birthday presents and so on. They study their favourite sportsmen and stars. But if you were to ask — Why are we in this world? What will happen when we die? — they would admit that they had not begun to think about it. Yet this is far more important than all these other things. No wonder God calls such people fools.

Rich toward God. Do our lives race unthinkingly on

towards the last day of life — that day of humiliation? Suppose we feel that we are rather like the rich fool, and we begin to realise how stupid this way of living is — is there any hope for us? The Lord Jesus called to Himself people who realised that they were poor and foolish in God's eyes. He died on the cross so that He might give us real riches by bringing us to know Him. Remind the children that we are here in this world for only a short time. What really matters is how we look in God's holy sight. The Lord Jesus Christ is waiting for us to turn to Him in repentance so that He can prepare us for that great day when we shall be summoned before Him. If we have asked Him to forgive us and make us His own children, then on that day we shall be greeted by Him and taken into eternal Paradise.

Older children can be engaged by a review of various human accomplishments which are useless when the soul is taken. What use is power, great learning, athletic cups, etc? Show how even on earth these things do not make people happy. Even some millionaires commit suicide. And what use are these things when we go to stand before God?

Visual Aid

Pictures cut from glossy magazines of luxury houses and expensive possessions will help the children see the modern equivalent of this rich fool. Drawings of his barns, showing acres of farmland stretching into the distance, will also help the children remember this vivid parable. A sign 'BANKRUPT' to be pinned across the pictures towards the end of the lesson will help make the point.

The Lost Coin (73) 10/5/08

Luke 15.8-10

Aim: To emphasise the lovingkindness of the Lord in seeking and saving lost and worthless sinners like us.

Teachers' Introduction

The three parables of *Luke 15* have often been cited as providing the perfect balance between God's initiatory role in our salvation and the sinner's all-important response. The Lord Jesus shows here how God begins the search for a lost

sinner even before he is aware of it, and how the Lord als
all that is necessary to accomplish salvation. The third o.
parables, that of the lost son, shows the prodigal making
personal response in shame and repentance. (As we relate each
parable, we shall succeed better if we bear the other two in
mind.)

Lesson Outline

Try to create the sensation of being *lost* in the children's
minds. Ask if — as small children — they ever had the
experience of realising they were lost. Perhaps they became
detached from their parents on a crowded beach and discovered
with horror that they were lost! With no money, no help and no
friends the situation was very frightening. What relief they felt
as they heard their mother's voice calling from another direction. Or perhaps at some time they have looked into their purse
or pocket for a precious banknote only to make the sickening
discovery that it had gone. They will recall the tears and fears as
they feverishly searched everywhere for the lost money.

Go on to explain that the Lord Jesus told three parables about
the lost. As they may expect, each of these parables had a
meaning. The first parable was about a man who lost a sheep;
the second about a woman who lost a coin; and the third about a
son who was lost to his father. We start with the second.

A worried woman. Tell the class about the woman and her
lost coin. It is possible that it may have been a valuable coin
given to the woman at the time of her marriage (as part of a
head-dress). However it is more likely to have been a large part
of her housekeeping (the equivalent of a day's wages). This was
a large sum for an ordinary household. (Think of one-fifth of
someone's weekly pay.)

Describe her patient and meticulous search, even into the
darkest corners of the house. All the time that she was
desperately trying to find it, new worries were springing up in
her mind. What would her husband say? How would she
manage to buy all the food and other necessities? From time to
time she probably sat down and cried, but then she would start
all over again, her broom reaching even further into every nook
and cranny.

The coin found. Picture her with her lamp suddenly coming across a tiny glint of metal, which turned out to be the little coin. Probably it was tarnished and at first hardly recognisable. But this did not bother the woman. She was full of relief and joy from the moment of its discovery. Soon the coin was washed, polished and polished, and placed on the mantelshelf, and she was off to gather her neighbours to tell them of her relief.

Lost sinners. Surprise the children by showing them that the Lord Jesus used this parable of a lost coin to describe us. Encourage them to recognise the likenesses. (Teachers should select the points most profitable for their age group. Younger classes will manage fewer than older classes.)

(1) Noticed. Remind them that there are millions of people in God's world — just as there are millions of coins. When you see a great crowd (eg: at a football match) you may wonder what value each person has. Yet just as this coin was precious to the woman, so the Bible tells us that God values each one of us, and is concerned about us. How amazing that God, to Whom we must look like little specks, knows all about each one of us.

(2) Tarnished. Suggest also that just as the silver coin doubtless became dirty and unrecognisable as it lay hidden away somewhere in a dark corner amongst the dust and dirt, so our sin has taken us away from God and spoiled us. Instead of living lives worthy of our Maker, we are corrupted by our sins, and barely recognisable as people made by Him. Yet, just as the woman went looking for the grubby little piece of metal, so *while we were yet sinners, Christ died for us (Romans 5.8).*

(3) Worthless. Remind the class that a coin, however valuable, is worth *nothing* when it is lost. No shopkeeper will exchange goods for money we have lost! The lost coin was of no use to the woman who owned it. We too are of no value to our Maker and Owner. We are useless and worthless to God because of our sinful hearts and deeds. We cannot be used by Him; we are not in His keeping or care.

(4) A great search. Explain feelingfully that as the woman searched energetically for her coin, so the Lord God went to great lengths to recover lost, worthless sinners and to bring them into His keeping. He sent His Son into this world of sin and shame to save us and restore us. Only by giving His life for

Cut out 4 large card circles. Copy these pictures onto 3, and write the words as shown on the reverse. On the fourth, write 'Sinners', and 'Found by the Saviour' on the back.

FRONT

(1) Lost Coin - found by the woman

(2) Lost Son - found by his father

Sinners

Lost Sheep - found by the shepherd

(3)

Found by the Saviour

BACK

VA 7 — Visual Aid for use with lessons on 'The Lost Coin', 'The Lost Sheep', and 'The Lost Son'.

us on the cross was it possible for the Lord Jesus Christ to cleanse away our sins and make us useful to Him.

(5) **Inanimate coins.** This parable highlights the woman's part in the restoration of her coin. Emphasise the point that the coin could not find itself! Nor could the coin help the woman to find it. It could not call out and tell her where it was! We need to be reminded that we are helpless sinners, utterly unable to *earn* our way to Heaven, to atone for our own sins, or to give ourselves new lives. We are dependent entirely upon the mercy and power of the Lord to save us.

(6) **Her tools.** Older classes might like to consider parallels for the woman's broom and candle. The apostle Peter speaks of God's Word — *to which you do well to pay attention as to a lamp shining in a dark place (2 Peter 1.19)*. It is the Gospel of Christ alone which brings light and understanding to our lost and darkened souls. The Gospel shines — telling us about Calvary, and the need of forgiveness and new life.

The broom, at first, must have seemed unkind to the coin, poking and prodding it about. This reminds us of how the Holy Spirit has to prod our conscience, and brush away our pride before we come to our senses and see our need of salvation. No person has ever come to the Lord to experience real conversion without being made aware of and ashamed of his sins.

(7) **Restored.** Just as the woman picked up her coin, cleaned it, and held it tightly, so repentant sinners have the experience of being 'ransomed, healed, restored, forgiven' by the Lord. They are given the assurance of knowing that they are now His valued possession, held in His hand, and used in His service.

(8) **God's joy.** Above all, this parable teaches us God's joy when a sinner is found. Even the angels of Heaven celebrate. Help the children to learn with amazement that there is rejoicing in Heaven when they — poor, insignificant sinners — return to the Saviour.

Remind the class of how they have frequently heard the Lord calling to them at Sunday School. Urge them to yield to the Saviour. Not only will this cause great rejoicing in Heaven but it will bring greater joy to them than anything else in this whole world.

> Lo, a loving Friend is waiting,
>   He is calling thee;
> Listen to His voice so tender,
>   'Come to Me.'

Visual Aid

VA 7 (see page 127) suggests a way of drawing together these 'lost-found' lessons in a simple but memorable way.

The Lost Sheep (74)

Luke 15.3-7

Aim: To emphasise our sinfulness in ever going astray from such a wise and kindly Shepherd. To demonstrate the lengths to which He went to rescue us, and to describe the joy with which He finds us.

Lesson Outline

Tell the class that the Bible often compares people with sheep (eg: *Isaiah 53.6*). This may seem surprising and not very flattering. If we must be pictured by animals, men and women would rather be represented by kingly lions, swift gazelles, gentle doves or other intelligent, attractive or perhaps powerful creatures. There is nothing glamorous about sheep, but as God looks down from Heaven, and sees our foolish behaviour, He sees the likeness.

Weak, foolish and vulnerable. Sheep are weak — compared with many other animals. They need a shepherd to watch over them and lead them to green pastures by day, and to protect them by night. Sheep are foolish and apt to wander off. Because the area where they are grazing is pleasant and well-pastured, they imagine that everywhere else is just the same. They do not realise that their present safety is due to the work of the shepherd who plans for them. They are easily tempted to leave the safety of the flock and wander off alone. They forget that, unlike the shepherd, they have no knowledge of the region around them, or of its pitfalls and dangers.

Sheep are highly vulnerable once they escape the protective care of the shepherd. Wild animals and even birds attack them.

Steep precipices and waterlogged ground are dangers they cannot cope with. There are also human enemies – thieves who will seize a lone and obviously lost sheep.

Comparisons. Point out that the Bible's use of sheep to picture human beings contrasts sharply with the ideas we are given by the television programmes of today. These persuade us that we must decide everything for ourselves, and that we are very capable and secure, needing no help or guidance from God. Are they right? They are obviously *wrong*! The moment we take our eyes off the television screen and take a good look at the world around us, we see how accurate God's assessment is. The world at large, and so many individual lives are in such a mess! There is so much misery and failure. Human beings *are* like sheep.

We do need someone wiser than ourselves to show us the way. We are surrounded by all kinds of danger. Satan is invisible to us, but he is the thief of human souls, who will take us as far away from God as possible. Like wandering sheep, we reject all the care of the supreme Shepherd and we head off on our own. Soon we fall into a deep gully, or into a deep, fast river (these things picturing temptation and sin) and we cannot get out. Or, wandering far away we find ourselves in a place where there is nothing much to eat, and we starve. This illustrates what happens when – as unbelievers – we have no food for our *souls*. We do not understand God's Word, and our souls starve. We try to feed on the entertainment of this present world, but inside us there is a hungry, shrivelled and dying soul. We are cut off from God, and ready to die eternally.

The sheep is saved. For the sake of the children adapt Christ's teaching to narrative form. Tell the class of a particular sheep that went astray. Ninety-nine were safely grazing in the open pasture but one was missing. The foolish creature had left the safety and security of the flock and set out on its own, only to fall into trouble, to starve, and to face death.

Describe the Eastern shepherd who, noticing that one sheep was missing, immediately made plans to go searching out in the wilderness until he found it. No doubt it was hard and dangerous to search in that mountainous region. Perhaps it took many days. His life was in danger as wild animals approached or rocks slipped from beneath his feet. But he persevered until, at last, he heard the pathetic bleat of his sheep. Tenderly he picked it up from the pit into which it had fallen. Carefully he examined it, then lifted it on to his strong, broad shoulders to carry it home. The homeward journey was swift and downhill compared with the outward struggle, and the shepherd was now a happy man.

A happy ending. You might imagine that this was the end of the story, but the main point which Jesus made was about the rejoicing which took place on the shepherd's return. As soon as he returned, he passed the good news to all who lived around. Before long his friends and neighbours were gathered, and joy and laughter rang across the valley as the shepherd invited them to: *Rejoice with me, for I have found my sheep which was lost!* This point says so much about the amazing compassion and kindness of God — that He *so feels* for unworthy, headstrong, arrogant human beings who spurn Him, that He not only pays an infinitely high price to save them from disaster, but rejoices greatly as each saved person is brought into His kingdom. Our rulers and the highly-ranked people of *this* world do not even know who we are! Would they care deeply about *our* problems, or pay a heavy price to help us? The pop stars, sports stars, and others who we may regard so highly — would they give up their wealth and comforts to help us? How can we reject the Almighty God of Heaven, Who sees us, knows about us, feels for us, and goes to such lengths to save us?

The Lord Jesus Christ is our Good Shepherd, for He left His Father's home in Heaven and came down to earth — *to seek and to save that which was lost (Luke 19.10)*. He sacrificed His life in order to rescue us from sin. Remind the children — especially older classes (who may have the impression that conversion is a hard step and that repentance is difficult) that becoming a Christian is like asking the Lord to lift us upon His shoulders, and take us into His keeping and kingdom. The day we first belong to Him is the greatest day of our lives.

A warning. Before closing the lesson, draw the children's attention to the Pharisees and the scribes who caused Jesus to tell this parable. In their pride they did not see themselves as lost sheep. They believed that God was well pleased with them and their religious activities, and they had no compassion for the sinful people who had come to listen to the Lord. Indeed, they criticised the Saviour for having anything to do with such people.

By telling this parable the Lord Jesus warned these smug hypocrites that unless they recognised themselves as sinners needing forgiveness and restoration, they would never cause the angels in Heaven to rejoice. Urge any self-satisfied children in your class to give up their pride, and to humbly admit that they are lost sheep, without any hope of Heaven unless they cry out to the Saviour to save them. How vital it is to be genuinely converted and able to say —

> *I will sing the wondrous story*
> *Of the Christ Who died for me;*
> *How He left His home in glory,*
> *For the cross on Calvary.*
> *I was lost: but Jesus found me —*
> *Found the sheep that went astray;*
> *Threw His loving arms around me,*
> *Drew me back into His way.*
> （Francis Rawley）

The Lost Son (75)

Luke 15.11-24

Aim: To follow step by step the Saviour's portrayal of sinful rebellion, and His description of a true conversion.

Teachers' Introduction

These lesson notes provide two separate outlines, the first for very young children, and the second for older classes. Teachers are asked to note carefully the difference in approach, because the methods outlined can be applied throughout the series. (See also — teachers' introduction to this series on page 119.)

Lesson Outline — For Younger Children

Relate the *whole* parable (without interruption for application) as vividly as possible, aiming to achieve the following:-

(a) *Appreciation* of the kind, good and generous character of the father.

(b) *Horror* and *disgust* at the behaviour of his younger son who selfishly demanded his share of the father's will, went as far away as possible and squandered it on himself. Help the children to see what a callous and greedy person the son was.

(c) *Pity* for the prodigal when events caught up with him and he found himself reduced to such squalor.

(d) *Relief* and *approval* when at last the son came to his senses and made his way home in shame, hoping that his father would accept him as a servant.

(e) *Amazement* that the father, instead of being angry, was not only prepared to take him in, but rejoiced at his safe return, and gave him a dignified place in his household.

Application. Proceed to explain the parallel Gospel facts, the hearts and concerns of the children having been awakened by the parable.

(a) Speak of the Lord God Who made this world, and gave every good and perfect thing in it. As you speak the children should begin to feel *appreciation* of the Lord's goodness.

(b) Speak then of how boys and girls (and grown-ups) want to forget all about God, keep away from His house, give no thanks to Him for all His gifts, and have nothing to do with Him in their lives. Describe how lots of people use God's gifts just to please themselves (eg: food to be greedy with, etc). Help the children to view this attitude and behaviour with *horror* and *disgust*.

(c) Tell the children where a godless, selfish life leads. Describe how people who live without God are nearly always unhappy, especially when life becomes hard and difficult. Draw out the children's *pity* for the unbeliever in these tragic circumstances. Point out that we are all in this sad state before we return to our heavenly Father.

(d) Ask them what is the best thing to do when we realise that we have sinned against God, and are a long way from Him. Encourage a sense of *relief* as you tell them that it is possible to pray to God, and to tell Him how sinful and wrong we have been. God wants us to ask for His forgiveness and to humbly offer to serve Him throughout life.

(e) Explain that God, instead of sending us away from His presence for ever and ever as we deserve, not only welcomes us back, but forgives us and makes us members of His own family. Speak of this with a due sense of *amazement*, and ask the children if they have ever prayed to God with shame and sorrow, and asked for His forgiveness. Urge them to do so, and to live close to Him for the rest of their days.

Lesson Outline – For Older Children

With this group we shall apply the parable step by step: –

(1) **Leaving a kind father.** We must make clear that the prodigal had no cause to be discontented with his father's house. (As we see from his attitude when he repented, his father's house was a place of plenty and kindness – even for the servants.) The father obviously represents God, Who is the *perfect* Father. So we begin the parable by speaking of the God Who made the world and all its resources for mankind to enjoy. God has given rich gifts to us, including our personal gifts – our faculties and abilities. Mention certain individual talents and powers, mental and athletic, which are distributed to people by God. Mention also the daily provisions that all enjoy. Point out the ingratitude of the prodigal, who behaved as though he just wished his father dead. 'All I want from you,' he said, 'is what I would have at your death!' What a picture this is of our attitude to God. We do not want *Him* – only the things He gives us.

(2) **Life in the far country.** When the father let him take away his share of the family wealth, he went to a country as far away as he could get, where he would hear nothing more from his father, and where his lifestyle could be the very opposite of the behaviour and values that his father held dear. Here again is a picture of us as sinful people! We wish there was no *heavenly* Father. We just want our abilities and our life for ourselves! Then we live as differently as we can from the holy and good standards desired by the Lord. We go far away from God, and if something reminds us of Him we stifle our conscience, switch on some music, watch a video or do something else to take our mind off the subject.

But all too soon the son was left with nothing. His money was spent. It is the same with us. We think life will be great without God, doing whatever we want; but soon worldly pleasures no longer satisfy us, and besides this, our years and our health (like the prodigal's wealth) run down, and life soon draws to its end. When things were sad enough, the prodigal faced yet another trial – famine. The once-rich heir was forced to survive as a keeper of pigs. Only now did he 'come to his senses'.

(3) The prodigal's heart is stirred. It was not until this point that the prodigal realised that his life away from his father was a disaster, and that he had been an arrogant fool. He learned also that no one in that far country cared about his problems. Ashamed and hungry he made up his mind to return home.

(4) The way back. Picture the son returning on foot, half-starved, to beg his father's forgiveness. Explain that he carried in his mind a carefully prepared and rehearsed speech which he hoped would quell his father's anger. In it he would fully admit his guilt towards God and his father, accepting that he no longer had any right to be treated as a member of the family. He would simply beg to be taken back as a servant.

Encourage children who are seeking the Lord to turn to these words in *Luke 15.18-19* for a simple but most helpful prayer of repentance. It helps us see that we must feel really ashamed of our behaviour towards our heavenly Father. We must admit our great sin, and ask Him to take us back, forgiving us, and allowing us to be His servants.

Imagine how dispirited the son must have felt as he started his journey. He had a long, long way to travel (from the far-away country). He began to realise that in his weak state he would never make it.

A great welcome. The surprising and exciting point in the parable is that the father saw him and went out to meet him while he was still a *great way off* (*AV*). The meaning is this: we sinful people could never reach God, left to ourselves. We depend on the fact that the Lord Jesus came out (from His heavenly home) to us, to rescue and save us. *He* has bridged the mighty gap caused by our sin. The Saviour came from Heaven to die at Calvary to bridge that gulf. Each person who truly repents and pleads for forgiveness like the prodigal can be forgiven by God *because* God has come to earth to meet us! Calvary's cross is pictured here, by the father coming to take his son home.

Stress this happy but unexpected ending to the parable. Instead of turning his son away, the father felt compassion as he saw the pathetic state to which he had been reduced. The father ran and embraced him. Then, as the son made his speech of sorrow and repentance, the father ordered his servants to fetch

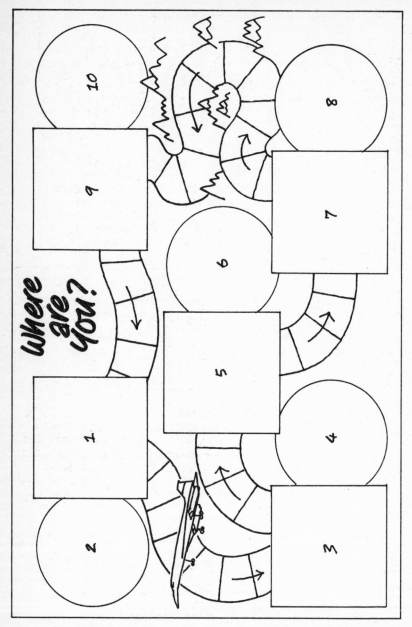

VA 8 – Visual Aid for use with Lesson 75 – 'The Lost Son'.

1

At the
REBELLIOUS
STAGE
-are we dreaming of
getting away from
the Lord & His
influence? 2

3

Living
in the
FAR COUNTRY
-are we enjoying
life
away from
God? 4

5

Suffering a
FAMINE
-are we experiencing
pain and
disappointment
from this
world? 6

This visual aid is
like a 'Board game'
showing the route
the Prodigal son
took. Copy out
the map on the
opposite page,
onto stiff card.
Draw these
picture squares
and application

7

9

Thinking
hard in the
PIGSTY
-are we coming to
our senses and
wishing we could
return to God? 8

A
WELCOME HOME
-are we overwhelmed
by God's lovingkindness
to such an
undeserving
sinner? 10

circles the same size as the shapes on the map.
The aircraft is to illustrate the meaning of 'a far
country.' As the lesson proceeds place the
shapes on their respective numbers.

a new outfit and the family ring. This indicates that the father not only forgave the prodigal, but restored him as a full member of the family.

Describe to the children the great joy of conversion and the powerful change which takes place. No sooner have we sincerely turned away from sin and started to frame our prayer, than we experience the great love of God for us. We are made members of His own family and receive: (a) a new nature (family likeness); (b) close contact with God as Father of the household; and (c) a place for ever in Heaven.

As you close the lesson, be very practical and ask your children which stage of the parable they have reached, for every human being is at one point or another of this parable.

(1) Are you at the rebellious stage — thinking of deserting God, your Maker and Father, in order to get away and enjoy the world?

(2) Are you still in the far country — living as far away from the Lord as possible and wasting your life and gifts?

(3) Are you beginning to feel like the prodigal in the pigsty — experiencing pain and disappointment with life, and wishing you could find the Lord?

(4) Are you ready to turn heavenwards — believing that God will come to your rescue and enable you to reach Him?

(5) Have you repented and returned — and found that the Lord has come to you, and embraced you by converting your life?

Visual Aid

VA 8 (see pages 136-137) represents in graphic form the various stages of the prodigal's journey and highlights the above questions so that teachers can help children to identify their own spiritual position.

The Grand Banquet (76)

Luke 14.16-24; see also Matthew 22.1-14

Aim: To help the class see that the reasons which people generally give for not believing God and seeking Him are only excuses.

Teachers' Introduction

This is a parable of great contrasts. On the one hand there is the king, or wealthy man, who is prepared to go to great lengths to provide this fabulous banquet for many people. On the other hand we see the insulting behaviour of those who refuse the invitation with the flimsiest of excuses. We therefore have the opportunity to extol the gracious generosity of the King of kings to undeserving sinners, and at the same time to show how people insult their Maker.

It should be a great encouragement to us to know that in this generation, in which the vast majority of the adult population scornfully refuses the Gospel, the Lord God is willing to open the doors of His kingdom to the young. Even many evangelical Christian organisations seem to doubt the possibility of real conversion amongst children, but we take literally the invitation of the Lord Jesus — *Permit the children to come to Me, and do not hinder them, for the kingdom of God belongs to such as these.* In the course of this lesson we shall take the part of the servants in the parable in issuing an invitation to the young.

Lesson Outline

Remind the class that in every day and age, including our own, the social standing of a person may be assessed by the kind of invitations he receives. Some adults will pay hundreds, even thousands, of pounds for a ticket which enables them to attend a dinner-party where they will rub shoulders with royalty, or with showbusiness personalities or international sportsmen. On the occasion of a royal or presidential wedding the invitations will be sent to an honoured few — the cream of society. At the coronation of Queen Elizabeth II a small number of places along the route were allocated to London schoolchildren. There was great competition for these few, favoured tickets, and headteachers chose their best behaved pupils for this rare privilege.

An invitation snubbed! Having set the scene in a modern way, turn back to the nobleman of *Luke 14* (no doubt rich and famous) who planned a great dinner-party for the elite of his town. In those days an initial invitation was issued in advance. Then, as the time of the feast drew near, a second invitation finally summoned the privileged guests to come. Imagine the surprise of the host's servants when they called on guests with these final invitations, and found that they did not want to attend. Even worse, imagine their amazement to hear the feeble excuses!

Excuse 1 – 'I have bought a piece of land and I need to go out and look at it.' Show the children how pathetic and dishonest this excuse appears the more we consider it. Why did this man have to go and look at his piece of land? He had undoubtedly seen it already, and if he had not, he had now paid for it. What difference would looking make? If he had made a bad bargain no amount of looking could alter or improve matters. Most probably he wanted to go and gloat over his latest possession. He put his personal pleasure before his obligation to keep his appointment at the feast, and his excuse was really his *choice*. He *preferred* to gloat over his possessions than to share the company of the rich host.

Excuse 2 – 'I have bought five yoke of oxen, and I am going to try them out.' Again we can see what a foolish excuse this was. Like the man who bought the land, he had probably seen them already. And if not, why not send a servant to test the oxen? Or why not delay testing until *after* the feast? The oxen would not have minded! This man's excuse appears more like an insult – 'I consider my business, my routine to be much more important than you and your feast!' Of course, though the refusal was rude, it was put in a polite way: 'Please consider me excused.' But polite words cannot disguise an insulting attitude. Older classes might like to think of an equivalent excuse for our day and age – 'I have bought a new car and want to try it out. My new computer needs programming so I can't come.'

Excuse 3 – 'I have married a wife, and for that reason I cannot come.' This begs the question, 'Why not?' No doubt the new wife would be welcome too. And in any case, she would surely have been pleased for him to go. It would have been more honest for this man to have said, 'I *will* not come,' instead of, 'I *cannot* come.' He blamed his family, but *he* was the one who did not want to go. So it was that these privileged people turned down the chance of a lifetime and insulted their gracious host with these hopeless excuses. Notice that they preferred to give *all* their time to their possessions, their businesses and their

families – just like so many people today, when God calls them
to worship Him.

Describe how angry the king was when he heard the excuses.
But he was determined to have this great banquet. The servants
were sent out to the houses of the poor, and to the places where
the crippled, blind and lame lived, and all were invited, until at
last the banquet hall was ringing with the excited clamouring of
people who previously had only seen the outside of the
mansion. They had come just as they were, without rich
clothing or money or anything else, to enjoy the riches of the
lord's feast.

We can imagine that as the feast got under way, and the
aroma of roast oxen and other meats wafted across the fields,
accompanied by the sounds of musical entertainment, some of
those who were formerly invited might have changed their
minds and decided to go along after all. If so, they would have
been deeply disappointed, and found that instead of a respect-
ful welcome, a guard had been posted at the door to keep them
out (v 24). The nobleman was determined that none of them
should now be allowed in.

Another invitation. Turn now to the great invitation of the
Lord, the general call of the Gospel addressed to all, and
describe how many people today refuse this invitation. When
we knock on their doors and invite them to Sunday School and
church services they are either scornful or they make excuses.
Ask the children some of the excuses which are given. Show
how similar they are to those in the parable. 'I am too busy.'
(Never too busy for television but too busy for spiritual life!)
'I've got a new car and want to take the family out.' 'I have to
visit my parents this Sunday.' 'I am far too busy to come to
church.' 'I've been picked for the football team,' etc.

Other excuses. This lesson could be an opportunity for
teachers of older classes to explain that other (more sophis-
ticated) reasons for not believing in God and worshipping Him
are also only excuses dressed up to sound good. 'I cannot believe
in a God Who allows wars, suffering, and death,' is an example.
This can easily be shown to be a weak excuse, especially from
people who are not interested in hearing any explanation of the
problem. It is obvious that they are putting up a barrier to shut
themselves off from God, and not sincerely trying to find

answers. All such things (wars, sicknesses, etc) come because we have sinned against God, and as rebels we are cut off from His help. Another common excuse is – 'I can't believe in God because science has proved He doesn't exist.' But of course, science has not proved this at all. On the contrary, many leading scientists around the world believe in God.

The day of judgement. Warn the children that those who make excuses in order to reject the Lord's invitation to be forgiven and converted will find themselves barred from Heaven (just like the insulting people who rejected the nobleman's invitation). Proud, self-righteous, selfish and greedy people, who see no need of a Saviour here, will be horrified to find themselves shut out from God's eternal kingdom.

God's great banquet. Describe the great feast which God has prepared for all those who *do* answer His invitation. Tell your class what it is to know the Lord of lords and King of kings as your own Saviour and Friend. Explain to them that He becomes our personal Guide through life, and day by day He gives us joy which non-Christians never know. Show how He uses even sorrows and griefs to our lasting benefit. Then show how He has prepared a wonderful home for us in Heaven so that death no longer frightens us. What a feast! Urge the children to listen to the voice of the Saviour and answer willingly, gladly and thankfully.

His gracious invitation. Now present the situation of the poor, maimed and blind who were finally invited to the feast. They had no 'right' to go; they owned no land (an important qualification in those days for obtaining invitations to social functions). They may even have suffered from illnesses and infectious diseases. They would certainly in many cases have been dirty and unkempt, and some disfigured also. They were dressed in simple, clumsy, threadbare clothes, and many were in rags. They were just not fit to go. Here is the application: – in God's sight our sin is ugly; our natures are deformed; and our deeds are like dirty rags. We own no 'land' as far as God is concerned – we have no virtues fit for the Lord, and deserve nothing. This part of the parable enables us to emphasise that the invitation is a *gracious* one. 'Grace' means something

absolutely undeserved and unmerited. God makes us fit and
worthy to come to Him by − (a) sending Christ to suffer, and
wash away our sins; and (b) renewing and changing our lives in
conversion. What an opportunity we have to explain these
things from this parable!

In describing the banquet as a feast of good things which
believers begin to enjoy at conversion, remember to emphasise
our present powerful blessings. Sometimes teachers give the
impression that the only result of conversion is that we go to
Heaven in the end.

The Good Samaritan (77)

Luke 10.25-37; Romans 5.6-10

Aim: To compare the Good Samaritan with the Lord Jesus
Christ, and to show how He can rescue us when other helpers
fail.

Teachers' Introduction

This parable was told by the Lord Jesus to answer a lawyer
who had come deliberately to trap him with a trick question. As
we follow the answers to the lawyer's questions, and examine
the parable of the Good Samaritan, we cannot but see a picture
of the Lord Jesus Himself. The *neighbour* described by Jesus
seems almost too good to be true, until we consider His own love
for poor, helpless sinners. Evangelicals down the centuries
have put this interpretation on the parable, and in Sunday
School work it gives us a wonderful opportunity to describe all
that the Saviour did for wounded sinners as He died on the cross
of Calvary. Point by point we can demonstrate how the Lord
Jesus can be equated with the Good Samaritan.

It must be acknowledged that this interpretation of the
parable has often been challenged by exegetes (including
Calvin, the prince of expositors). However, other giants in the
reformed tradition have upheld the approach we adopt here,
notably Luther, many of the English Puritans (Trapp typically
declares: 'This Samaritan is Christ'), Gill and Spurgeon. The
usual grounds for this interpretation are: (a) that the answer to
the lawyer's question demanded a *gracious* (as opposed to
'works') answer; and (b) that the parable clearly had a meaning

which would become fully clear to the lawyer as Christ — despised like a Samaritan — went to the cross in an attitude of compassion for others. On the basis of 'later fulfilled meaning' the lawyer would see that the parable was a picture of the Messiah's work. We pray that the Lord will plant this moving picture deeply into the children's minds.

Lesson Outline

Introduction. Ask your class if they know children who are good at asking 'clever' questions, or answering back at school. Point out that this is nothing new. Here we have a lawyer who wanted to trick the Lord Jesus by a clever question. Encourage your class to spot the way in which the Lord Jesus dealt with this man and left him silent and thoughtful.

The lawyer asked his carefully planned question. He wanted to hear an answer which he would then criticise and find fault with. To his surprise Jesus did not give an elaborate answer. Instead He turned the question back to the man. This made the lawyer look rather silly, as the question was such a simple one. The lawyer gave the correct answer, and in an effort to cover his embarrassment quickly devised another question. He was a proud man, who knew God's laws, and was sure that he kept them.

Again he was surprised by the way the Lord Jesus responded to this second question. The lawyer thought he deserved eternal life because he knew so much, and because of his good standing in society, but the Lord Jesus knew his heart. The Saviour knows our hearts too. You may tell your Sunday School teacher that you trust in God, but God sees into your heart and He knows if you really do.

How do you know if a girl or boy is really a Christian? Is it because they *say* they love God, or know the ten command-ments, and come to Sunday School each week? Jesus told the lawyer a story which put him to the test. He showed the proud lawyer that people who really love God, who have been truly converted, show it in their behaviour.

Those who really know the kindness of the Lord Jesus, cannot help showing it to others. However, there was a deeper meaning in the Lord's parable, for He also gave a picture of His own concern for lost and sinful people, and how He would save their souls.

The parable. It would be wise to explain at the beginning that the two main characters in this story belonged to enemy nations. Jews and Samaritans hated each other. Although the parable was told to Jews, the hero of the parable was a Samaritan who turned out to be much better than the Jews. Imagine the surprise of those who listened (and perhaps their anger also). The Lord prepared them to understand that someone despised and rejected would turn out to be *their* Saviour. (Note: in these notes (a) refers to the telling of the parable, and (b) refers to the spiritual application or meaning.)

A journey. (a) Describe the Jew setting off on the lonely, mountainous road to Jericho. Maybe he had some very valuable things loaded on his donkey and we can try to picture him setting out, hoping to reach an inn before nightfall.

(b) Introduce your class to a second kind of traveller – *they* are travelling on the road of life. Explain that every man, woman and child is on a journey from birth to death. The whole of life is like a journey, and we would all like it to be enjoyable and to have a happy ending.

Attacked. (a) Jesus' words are very graphic: *He fell among robbers, and they stripped him and beat him, and went off leaving him half dead* (v 30). Not content with robbing the man, they nearly murdered him too. This was a very vicious and violent attack. The poor man was left with nothing.

(b) Tell the class that before we have gone very far on life's journey, we are attacked. Instead of growing from a happy childhood to a pleasant, worthwhile adulthood, living as God intended, we are attacked by all kinds of evil. Satan snatches away any belief and trust we may have in the Lord. We are soon overwhelmed and injured by the lies, the hatred, the pride and the filth of this world. Our 'innocence', our honesty and our character are soon stripped away, and before long we lie open and exposed to all the devil's temptations. When God looks down upon us He sees us resembling the poor, wounded man on the side of the road. We are dying – never to reach the end of life in the happy way we desired – and there is nothing we can do to save ourselves.

Ignored. (a) The poor, dying Jew may have dimly seen the Levite and priest who came that way, hoping they would help him. They were, after all, fellow Jews and professional ministers of the church. But having seen what a state he was in, they passed by on the other side.

(b) Explain that often when people are disappointed, unhappy and even desperate, they look for help from various measures which claim to impart happiness. They turn to getting wealth or possessions, to drink, sport, entertainment, the pursuit of ambition, power or fame, and to religious ritual. But none of these can cure the problem of an empty soul. Often they leave their followers drained of money and abandoned to a worse condition than before.

An enemy. (a) The next footsteps to approach were those of a Samaritan. The dying man had no hope of help from him. Why, he himself had often insulted Samaritans. Now that he was lying in the 'gutter' in a horrifying condition he expected nothing more than to be jeered at as the Samaritan approached.

(b) The only Person Who is able to help wounded sinners is the Lord, but we have treated Him as an enemy. We have lived far from Him, flouted His laws and scorned His name. Can we expect Him to stop and help?

Unexpected help. (a) Tell how the Lord Jesus described, much to everyone's surprise, how the Samaritan felt pity for the Jew and came over to him, not allowing the blood and wounds to put him off. Nor did he consider the danger he was risking from a further attack. Instead he administered soothing oil and medicine to the wounds, and bound them with bandages, so that the man would survive. Then, at great inconvenience to himself, he lifted his patient on to his own animal, and took him to the nearest inn. Probably it was dark and cold by the time they arrived, but the Lord told how the Samaritan then *took care of him*, probably nursing him through the night.

(b) Encourage older classes to look at *Romans 5.6-10* which is a perfect commentary on this parable. It points out that while we were *still helpless*, Christ died for the ungodly, while we were *yet sinners* Christ died for us, and that while we were *enemies* we were reconciled and saved.

Help the class to appreciate the amazing love and compassion of Christ in coming down to earth to save people like us who hate Him. He came to deal with the wounds inflicted upon us by sin. He went to the cross of Calvary and did more for us than even the Samaritan did for the Jew. He allowed men to nail Him to the tree and then He suffered the punishment for every sin ever committed by those who become His people. He himself – *was wounded for our transgressions, he was bruised for our iniquities (Isaiah 53.5, AV)*. This means that He was wounded and bruised for our sins. He washed them away by giving His own life, His blood, so that we might be restored and forgiven.

The cost covered. (a) Explain that even this was not the end of the story. The following morning, before continuing his journey, the Samaritan paid the innkeeper the equivalent of two days' wages (teachers could indicate an appropriate figure) to continue nursing the wounded man back to health. He promised also to repay any further expenses incurred, on his return.

(b) Similarly the Lord Jesus not only paid the price to have our sins forgiven. He also provides us with the means to have our lives renewed so that we can go on our way rejoicing, certain that, because of His love, we shall safely reach Heaven. What more could we ask?

A new attitude. (a) Doubtless when the Jew regained consciousness and was told what had happened to him, he greatly changed his attitude towards Samaritans.

(b) Urge the children to review their attitude towards God, Who is ready to be their Saviour. Show them how wicked and ungrateful it would be to shun such wonderful grace and loving-kindness. As they begin to take in and appreciate what the Lord Jesus has done for them, suggest that they should want to obey and follow Him for the rest of their lives. Religion would then no longer be the proud self-righteousness of the Levite and priest, but a personal, heartfelt desire to please the Saviour – a great longing to share His love and mercy with everyone they know (their 'neighbours') and with all who need His help.

Visual Aid

Draw four figures to illustrate the Jew, a robber, the priest and the Samaritan. On the back of the outline figures mark the words 'Us', 'Life without God', 'Disappointments', and 'The Lord Jesus Christ' respectively. Use these throughout the lesson to draw the parallels.

The Rich Man and Lazarus (78)

Luke 16.19-31

Aim: To discover what happens to us after death from the only Person Who really knows.

Lesson Outline

Rich and poor. Using the visual aid, describe these two men who represent opposite extremes of society. Describe the rich man's mansion and clothing. Explain that purple could be afforded only by the very rich. Then ask the class if they can guess the kind of food he enjoyed, described in the parable as 'sumptuous' *(AV)*. Suggest that had he lived today he would probably have owned a Rolls Royce, a Bentley, a Ferrari, a Cadillac, etc. This man obviously spared no effort in providing himself with every luxury which life could provide. But he must have grown very selfish and hard, for just outside his gate lay the beggar Lazarus. Give a vivid description of Lazarus' sad condition from verse 21.

Something in common. Although these men lived so differently, we discover in verse 22 that the same thing happened to both of them: they died. Perhaps the rich man called in the best doctors that money could obtain, but still he died. Everyone without exception has to die, however rich or powerful or strong or famous. (Teachers may like to give some examples of wealthy or famous people who died when quite young.) Everyone has to die — but what happens after death? This is what we need to know more than anything else. Here the Lord Jesus, God's Son, tells us in picture form. Here is a unique opportunity to learn from the only authority on the subject. When death came to the two men in the parable, it placed an even greater difference between them.

(1) The unbeliever has no God. The rich man was buried (v 22). The last luxury that his money could secure for him was a grand funeral. Doubtless many people turned up. But as far as the rich man was concerned, it was at this point that his riches ran out. As he passed from this world into the next, he left behind all his wealth and comforts and power, and had to face

God and the truth about his life. In life he had no time for God or His ways, and now, as a result, he was condemned to spend eternity away from Him. With horror and terror he began to realise what it was like to live in darkness and despair and under punishment. In life he had lived without worshipping or serving God, and yet he had feasted greedily on God's gifts to mankind. Now all God's gifts and blessings were withdrawn. The Lord Jesus described hell as a never-ending flame, which brings great thirst to its tormented prisoners.

(2) **No prayers answered.** The rich man's first reaction was to cry for help. In life he had always been able to buy relief for his pains. How tragic to think that he prayed for the first time when it was too late — for he was already in hell. Is some boy or girl in the class going to leave it too late? Will someone be terrified and horrified one day and shut away from God before he realises for the first time the value of his eternal soul?

(3) **No changing places.** But the rich man had more to learn. He was told by God's servant that there was a great chasm between Heaven and hell and no one could pass from one place to the other. This meant, first, that neither Lazarus nor anyone else could come to comfort him; and, secondly, that because life was now over it was too late for the rich man to seek God's forgiveness.

(4) **No end to punishment.** His last request was also rejected. Much of his horror once he was in hell seems to have been caused by his fear of the arrival — in due course — of his five brothers, who would no doubt hate him for all his misdeeds to them while he lived on earth. Perhaps he had been responsible for leading his friends and family on the pathway of sin. Now, the once-rich man wanted to prevent them from making his punishment in hell even worse! But it was pointed out that all men and women are given ample warning on earth. The Word of God *must* be listened to by everyone — for God has given no other messenger; no other religion.

What must we learn? According to the age of the class, children can be encouraged to draw the following lessons.

(a) Everyone must die. Show how idiotic it is not to prepare for this one certain event. Yet, like the rich man, most people make provision for everything except death. People take out insurance policies and even plan their funerals – but they make no provision for their eternal souls!

(b) If we live without God we must die without Him and spend eternity without Him. All the nice things in life will cease and we shall be left to our own selfish, twisted hearts, and the company of those like ourselves. The punishment of our sins will engulf us and there will not be any comfort to relieve the agony. There will be no more joy and laughter, no more love and friendship, no more beautiful or enjoyable things to take our minds off our wretched state. Hell is full of lies, hate, ugliness and despair. Try to describe in some way the experience of waking up in a new and horrifying realm after death.

(c) At death God's offer of forgiveness closes. It will be too late to ask for His mercy, and He will have to take away all His blessings from us.

(d) We shall be responsible not only for taking ourselves to hell, but for leading others there too. We shall realise how many warnings God has given us through the Bible and through His people and how unbelievably foolish we were to ignore these (v 31).

Death for believers. As the class begins to appreciate the solemnity of the rich man's position, turn their minds to the position of Lazarus. We can be sure that he had repented of his sin and trusted in God for the salvation of his soul, because the Bible throughout tells us that only people who believe on the Lord can go to Heaven. Whether we are rich or poor makes no difference. Only the Lord Jesus Christ can make it possible for us to go to Heaven, and if we trust in Him and give our lives to Him, He has promised to take us to His heavenly home.

Lazarus received no burial. His disease-racked body was probably taken and placed in a pauper's grave. But by the time that happened, angels had already carried his soul to Heaven. What an adventure! He was taken into the comfort and love of Heaven, to enjoy being with the Lord, his Saviour, for ever. All sorrow and sadness had gone and he would never again know hunger or thirst or tears or pain (*Revelation 21.4*). Instead, he saw the Saviour and was made like Him, pure and without sin. He saw amazing sights – innumerable angels, scenes of breath-taking beauty, and all the great people mentioned in the

VA 9 — *Visual Aid for use with Lesson 78 — 'The Rich Man and Lazarus'.*

Bible — and he tasted the atmosphere of Paradise.

Our application should be obvious. Remind the children that God is warning them *now*, from His Word, not to follow the rich man to hell. Urge them not to delay. Death can come at any time and it will be too late then to seek mercy. We shall suffer the punishment of sin for ever. Remind them that the Lord has prepared a wonderful home in Heaven for His children. He pleads with us to forget the pleasures of this world, which pass away so quickly, and to set our hearts on the things above, which last for ever.

Younger children. We must not seek to *scare* little children away from hell, but yet we must present the facts. As with previous parables we will probably help them most by relating the parable simply and feelingfully before pointing out several simple, clear points from the above range of applications. A great number of people have been brought by the Holy Spirit to seek the Lord as children, through the earnest presentation of these facts. Let us go to the task with a great sense of responsibility and opportunity.

Visual Aid

VA 9 (see page 151) illustrates how the rich man and Lazarus changed places in the next world.

The Pharisee and the Publican (79)

Luke 18.9-14

Aim: To teach children the right way to approach the Lord, using the Lord's own tactic of surprise which He used when He taught about the kind of prayer which God hears.

Teachers' Introduction

This parable establishes with great simplicity that the only way to approach God is as a sinner needing His mercy. This will be an encouragement to children who have no religious pretensions but who would like to know the Lord. It will come as a warning to those who, like the Pharisee, think that God is pleased with their imagined goodness.

It is easy to underestimate the time needed for preparing this lesson. On the surface it seems such a simple one that we may be tempted to give it insufficient thought. This will lead to greater confusion in the children than before. We need to plan each step carefully, and be quite clear about our approach.

Lesson Outline

Introduction. Ask the children if God answers the prayers of everyone. The correct answer may well surprise them. Jesus spoke about two men who prayed to God, but the Lord only blessed one of them. Describe the two men in such a way that they remind the children of people today. Ask them to listen, and then tell you which prayer God answered.

The Pharisee. This man was very religious. He was frequently to be found at the synagogue, in a prominent place. He spent much of his life following every detail of the Jewish law, and he was determined that everyone should admire him for his devout life. Often he would stop to pray at street corners where people would see, and he made sure everyone knew that he gave money to the Temple. He even dressed in a way that would mark him out as a religious leader. He wore a part of God's law in a little box strapped to his forehead, and he dressed differently from other people. (See the visual aid depicting a Pharisee in *Lessons for Life*, Book 1, page 64.)

The publican. He was a man who in all probability had not worshipped God for a long time. He was not a publican in the sense that we use the word today — but a tax-gatherer. This did not make him popular with his fellow Jews but it made him rich. Most tax-gatherers were cheats, and the people despised them. This man could take more money than the Roman authorities required, and pocket the difference. Having gone to these lengths to get money, he spent it on himself. He did whatever he wanted, and had ignored the Lord — until this moment, when he suddenly went to the Temple to pray. Now which person do you think God listened to?

God is not impressed by status. Whatever answer the children give, show them that God does not listen to prayers simply because the person who prays them occupies some special or high place in society, or claims to be superior to others. Even if a man is a Prime Minister (or President), a famous sportsman or even a church leader, God does not hear his prayers just because he has that position. In this world *position* makes all the difference. But God is far more interested in the prayer itself, and the attitude of heart which lies behind the prayer.

What did these men pray? The Pharisee did not really pray to God at all. The Lord Jesus said he prayed *to himself*. He proudly went through a list of all his imagined good deeds, and thanked God he was not sinful like other people! Point out to the children the number of times the word 'I' appears in verses 11-12. The Pharisee was proud, and taken up with himself!

The tax-gatherer was entirely different. He dared not look up. Instead he turned his eyes to the ground and 'beat his breast' (for the people of those days expressed themselves with great feeling). As he did so he cried out – *God, be merciful to me, the sinner!* Now can we answer the question – Which prayer did God answer? The Lord Jesus tells us that He heard the second man's prayer.

Why one of the prayers was no good. The Pharisee was not really speaking to God; he was just telling himself how good he was. God does not listen to such prayers for He sees inside the heart of such a person, and sees it full of pride and conceit, jealousy and hatred. He sees a very nasty kind of sinner. Warn any 'show offs' in your class who are disgusted with the Pharisee, that it is possible for children to be 'mini-Pharisees'!

Did the class notice any other glaring fault with the Pharisee's prayer? It is very obvious. He did not actually pray for anything! He did not ask God for any blessing, and so the Lord did not answer his prayer. Nor will the Lord hear our prayers if we do not ask Him: (1) to forgive our many sins; (2) to change us and make us one of His children (if we are not yet converted); (3) to help us overcome the sins which grieve and hurt Him; and (4) to guide and instruct us day by day. No one can have prayers answered who does not want pardon, a new life, and to be governed and ruled by the Lord.

How pride was boosted. As an extra point, perhaps useful to older classes, it is good to draw attention to the Pharisee's technique for boosting his pride and self-righteousness. Instead of examining his life and his heart in the light of the standards which God provides, he compared himself with the very worst person he could see near him, the tax-gatherer, and it made him feel good. Show the class the technique from his words. People still do the same today. They think of people who commit the worst kinds of outward sin (murder, violence, swindling, etc), and tell themselves how much better they are. Even children preen themselves by contrasting themselves with others whose faults are more obvious. But the Lord looks on the *heart*. Explain the sinfulness and nastiness of heart sins – pride, jealousy, selfishness, hatred, deceitfulness, greed, and so on. We are all deeply sinful in God's sight and cannot expect Him to hear our prayers until we repent and ask His forgiveness.

The prayer that God answered. Explain that we do not know what had caused this tax-gatherer to enter God's house. Maybe some disaster had befallen him, or he had grown tired of his evil life, or he had begun to think of death. But as he entered God's house he realised that he had no right to speak to the holy God against Whom he had sinned so much. He could only beg forgiveness. By contrast with the Pharisee, he was *humble*, he felt *unworthy*, he was very *sincere*, and *he asked to be forgiven*. He realised that he must be condemned for his sin, and so he asked for *mercy*. The result was that he went home justified, forgiven and exalted (which means he was 'promoted' to being a child of God).

What can we learn?

(1) That no one is too bad or sinful to speak to God if he is really repentant.

(2) That God will hear our prayer if it is genuine and heartfelt, however short and simple it may be.

(3) That we cannot fool God. We cannot pretend to Him that we are good and sinless. He sees right into our hearts.

(4) That none of us can approach God or expect Him to answer our prayers until we have first asked for His mercy and forgiveness. No one deserves an audience with the Lord God, but because of His grace and mercy even the 'vilest offender who truly believes' can approach Him and find Him. Have you ever humbly seen yourself as a sinner and asked God's forgiveness?

The Pounds (80)

Luke 19.11-27

Aim: To prepare children for the coming of the Saviour.

Teachers' Introduction

Coming as it does toward the end of our series of parables, this parable will be especially useful because it describes the world in a state of rebellion before the return of the Lord. Many children must be tempted to despise Christianity because it is rejected by the mass of people today. This parable puts matters in perspective, for in it the Lord Jesus Christ, two thousand years ago, predicted that the world at large would reject the rule of God during His own 'absence' from the world, and that a large scale revolt against the Creator would be organised. The root cause of this rebellion would be the sinfulness of the human heart. By pointing these things out we show our classes that Christianity, far from failing, has a prophetic message which is being fulfilled before our eyes. At the end of the age Christ will return (just like the nobleman in the parable) to judge those who have rejected Him.

Lesson Outline

Introduction. Tell the class that we are going to hear about a nobleman who was such a great man that he was to be made a king. He had to leave his country to go to the land where he would be given his kingdom (just as certain kings of Israel went to Rome to receive this honour from Cæsar).

Teachers will be aware that there are several very different interpretations of this parable. A common approach is to assume that the money represents abilities which are given to people to use in service until the Lord returns. We advocate, however, the following time-honoured approach as the most natural. We see three classes of person spoken of here —

(1) The outright rebel against God.

(2) The person who trades with his money (this being a picture of 'investing' by faith the Gospel knowledge which God has given him — in other words, a believer is depicted).

(3) The person who hoards up his money, does nothing useful

with it (ie: who knows the Gospel, and ignores it), and is condemned in the last day.

(1) The rebels. While the king was gone (v 14) some of his people decided to rebel and set themselves up as rulers. They introduced their own laws and made a mockery of their king, just as some children stop work and fool around while their teacher is out of the class-room. These rebels were very foolish because they met with a terrible punishment when their king returned. Whatever they did in his absence did not alter the fact that he was their ruler and that they would eventually have to account to him for their conduct.

Why is our world in such a state of rebellion against God? The Lord Jesus Christ has returned to Heaven, and while He is away men and women turn against Him, sneer at His Church, and do as they want. They break His laws, they want nothing to do with His Word, and they will not worship Him. In this parable the Lord warned that this will not go on indefinitely. One day He will return to this world as King and Judge, and will have no alternative but to punish those who have rebelled.

(2) Those who acted. As we consider the giving of the money (v 13), we see how the nobleman gave special instructions to the ten servants, and how they responded. (These servants are not to be compared with the citizens at large.) Before the nobleman went away, he called in these servants and gave each of them a *pound (AV)*. (This pound was a *mina*, which was worth 100 *denarii*, nearly a third of a year's wages. It was a large sum of money.) They knew that he expected them to trade with the 'pound' and so make more money. Suggest to the class ways in which this might have been achieved, eg: buying seeds to grow to produce a marketable crop. To make use of the 'pound' would have shown respect for the giver, and a desire to please and obey him.

The money may be said to stand for God's Word and God's grace to man. Everyone has some knowledge of God; every child has some understanding or awareness that God exists. Everyone hears the voice of conscience. In addition, many children have obtained the knowledge of the Gospel (the way of salvation) through Sunday School, and other ways.

If that knowledge is believed and obeyed, then it will lead to much greater knowledge. *To everyone who has shall more be given*. It will be like money making more money! If a person is moved by his 'pound's-worth' of Gospel knowledge to repent and believe, he will receive more knowledge. Repenting and believing is investing the knowledge. As we humble ourselves before the Lord to seek Him as Saviour, then the result will be that our knowledge *and* experience of God will grow dramatically. We come to know the Lord through conversion. Then we grow as Christians. Of course, this can only happen as the result of the work of the Spirit of God. But the parable warns us never to abuse the little knowledge of the Gospel which we have, but to act upon it. Once a person is converted, the more he yields his life to the Lord in response to the blessings God gives him, the more God will use him and bless him.

(3) **The lazy servant.** What about the man who made no use of his money, and came up with disgraceful excuses? This man preserved the money and put it out of sight. The reasons which he gave for this action were so insolent and rude as to be unbelievable. He said he was afraid of the nobleman because he was such a hard taskmaster − a man who forced everything he could get from his servants, seizing everything which the tenant farmers worked to produce. This man hid away the 'pound' because he did not want to trade for the nobleman or get involved with his affairs.

The first sin of this man was that he made up his mind about the harsh character of the nobleman against all the facts. The nobleman was in fact absolutely kind, fair and reasonable, and gave amazingly generous rewards. Show the children that in the same way, men, women and children make up their minds that God is unfair and unreasonable. They decide that God makes unreasonable demands on people when He calls them to love and serve Him. They accuse God of unkindness and imagine that to be a Christian means becoming a miserable slave living a gloomy life without pleasures. They decide (like the man in the parable) that God is a hard taskmaster.

Young people must be shown that this foolish and hostile thinking insults God. Tell them that down the centuries all kinds of people − rich and poor, famous and unknown, brilliant and simple − have found the Lord to be the kindest Friend and Saviour possible. Explain that this lazy and hostile servant had his money taken away. It was given to another servant who would respect and make good use of it. Warn the class that those who ignore Gospel knowledge are in danger of having that advantage taken away, so that they are never again touched by the message.

So this parable shows us three classes of person: the outright rebel against God; the person who 'invests' the Gospel knowledge by repenting and trusting the Lord; and the person who smoulders against God and who never acts on the things he knows. Challenge the children to go home and seriously think, 'Which of these three am I like?'

Visual Aid

Make three mock banknotes: a one pound note, a five pound note, and a ten pound note. Using a felt-tip pen write on the reverse side of the notes as follows:

(1) On the one pound note: 'Given the Gospel, Resented God, Lost everything'.

(2) On both the five and ten pound notes: 'Pardon, New life, Understanding, Happiness'.

(3) On the ten pound note add: 'Service for Christ, Prayer answered'.

At the point in the lesson where the class is told of the distribution of the pounds hold up the one pound note. Tell how one man took his pound and hid it. Choose some suitable container and hide the note out of sight.

On reaching the point of the lesson where the successful servants are spoken of, illustrate your application with the other two notes. As you turn them round to show the words written on the back, you will be able to explain that all who invest their Gospel knowledge and come to Christ, find new life, pardon, clear understanding, and a new happiness. However, you will also be able to show that while all converted people experience these things, the Lord wants them to go on in the Christian life to trust Him and prove Him. The 'ten-pound' person has trusted and served Him more and has gained even more.

When you come to describe the excuses of the wicked servant, produce the one pound note from its place of conceal-ment. When you have shown how this attitude is like that of so many boys and girls, turn the note over to show the words — 'Given the Gospel, Resented God, Lost everything.'

A final note of warning – take care not to give the impression that salvation may be earned. With the 'trading' parable it is possible to fall into this trap unwittingly. *Using* the pound means *investing* Gospel knowledge – in other words, going earnestly to the Lord Jesus Christ in repentance, and depending on Him to pay the price of sin.

Younger classes. Teachers should follow the usual pattern. Instead of expecting the youngest ones to follow the telling and applying of the parable in stages (as above), tell the outline of the parable in an engrossing way, and then apply suitable points to their hearts afterwards. Describe how the kind nobleman set off to receive a great honour, leaving and trusting his servants with large sums of money to be used in his absence.

Describe the three categories: –

(A) The disgraceful rebels who seized their farms as soon as his back was turned. (The children should feel disgusted with this group.)

(B) The servants who worked hard in his absence and made good use of his money. (The children should admire these servants.)

(C) The lazy servant who hid and wasted the money. (The children should appreciate the foolishness of a missed opportunity.)

Next tell the class how the nobleman dealt with each category: Group (A) was punished; group (B) was rewarded; and (C) had his money taken away.

Three children and their responses. Tell them about three (sample) children who come to Sunday School. They hear about the kindness and love of God, Who provides us with all good things and invites us to trust the Saviour. Child (A) refuses to listen, hates the lessons and goes home not caring whether he breaks God's laws or not, and laughing at those who take His Word seriously. Child (B) listens carefully, wants to obey the Lord, is sorry for his sin and asks the Lord Jesus to forgive him. Child (C) comes to Sunday School, listens and remembers much of what the teacher has said, but goes home and does nothing about it. What will the Lord think of us if we behave like this?

The Barren Fig-Tree (81)

Luke 13.6-9

Aim: This parable enables us at the end of the series to challenge the children as to their own response to the Gospel parables they have heard. What good has been done to their souls? What effect have the lessons had?

Teachers' Introduction

This parable falls into the same category of lesson as that of the Sower and the Two Trees, but it has its own special emphasis, and is particularly appropriate at the conclusion of this series. The unique feature of this parable is that it tests not only the children's knowledge but also their response. (Teachers will find helpful personal preparation of this subject by reading *Isaiah 5.1-7*, where the Lord's reasoning is made plain.)

The vineyard and its owner. Describe an Eastern vineyard, often walled for protection against weather and thieves, and imagine it at harvest time with its rich crop of grapes. Then describe the vineyard owner — a wealthy man whose task was to ensure that his land was efficiently farmed for the benefit of his entire family and work-force. Older classes should by now recognise this as a picture of this world and of God its owner and sustainer. Mention that God made the world and everything in it *(Psalm 24);* that He created a garden for the first man and woman; and that He provides richly for all His creatures. We, in particular, have the privilege of hearing His Word Sunday by Sunday and of being shown the way of salvation.

The fig-tree — its expected fruit. Tell the class about the special attractions of a fig-tree: —

(a) They were one of the most fruitful trees available, bearing fruit *twice* every year. In the Holy Land the crop ripens first in June, and again from August to September. The promise of fruit comes when fruit-buds appear ahead of the leaves in February, and by the time the leaves have fully formed the fruit is ripe. Watching the fruit is one of the special enjoyments of the fig-tree.

(b) They could be expected to produce a crop of fruit even in their first year, but certainly in the second and third.

(c) The fruit was not only tasty and enjoyable, but health-promoting. It was used medicinally as a poultice for boils (eg: *2 Kings 20.7* and *Isaiah 38.21*).

(d) The fig-tree was something of a status symbol for its owner, a symbol of prosperity of which he could be proud. In the Holy Land fig-trees will grow up to 20 or 30 feet, and the trunk may attain 2-3 feet in diameter. It is a glorious and shade-providing tree to grow by a well, and such an arrangement indicated a successful vineyard.

Describe how the landowner, by now a successful producer, decided to plant such a tree in a special corner of his fertile vineyard, certain that it would be a beautiful, fruitful and worthwhile tree, and a special jewel in the vineyard. Remind the children that when the Lord God creates each human being, He has every right to expect a return for His love. We are, after all, made so distinct from the animals, and are capable of gratitude, worship, and intelligent love and service. Point out that *fruit* in the parable stands for behaviour and character in our lives. Show, therefore, that the Lord looks for belief in Himself, trust in His way of salvation, praise and love, obedience to His commands, and willingness to follow and serve Him.

The fig-tree – its failure. Picture the deep disappointment of the vineyard owner, when, after three years of patient waiting, he discovered that his fig-tree (which was to be his prize possession) still bore no fruit. He felt very let down, and even angry. He had acquired a perfect young tree. He had planted it in a most favourable place. It had been most carefully tended. Compare his feelings with the anguish and pain which we cause the Lord if we are useless to Him. Instead of being people who love, believe and obey Him, we behave as if He did not exist, and as if He had no right to our obedience, and no claim to our love. Instead of fruit, the Lord sees deceitfulness, selfishness, and unbelief all over us, like lank, diseased, yellowing leaves.

The owner's verdict. Ask the children what they would expect the disappointed owner to do. Justify his decision to cut the tree down. Clearly this useless tree was a waste of space, and a waste of time for the keeper of the vineyard. Emphasise the 'waste-of-space-and-time' aspect of sin and unbelief. What a waste to God are selfish and stubborn lives! How unbelievers love to enjoy and take in God's gifts of nature, health, food, memory, mind, talents, and so on, and to waste these treasures on themselves and never think of their debt to God!

If your class consists chiefly of children who have attended for some time and who ought by now to have made a response to the Gospel, but show no signs of doing so, then show how they resemble the fig-tree which was totally useless to its owner. Attending Sunday School and having a head knowledge of God's Word is useless without a real and personal response to the Lord, which alone leads to fruitful living.

The vineyard-keeper's plea. Explain that the fig-tree might well have been cut down and burnt immediately, except that the vineyard-keeper who was responsible for the care of all the plants, pleaded with the owner to give it one last chance. He also had reason to be frustrated by the fruitless tree on which he had personally spent a good deal of time and energy, but he suggested a course of action to rescue the tree from being cut down immediately.

The children ought to recognise that this vineyard-keeper represents the Saviour, Who, through the Gospel, gives people a chance to be changed, and to become worthwhile to the Father. Remind them that He was willing to give His life and suffer the pain and agony of Calvary so that people could be spared from judgement and punishment.

Help them to appreciate such tender and undeserved love and concern for their lives. After all, just as the vineyard-keeper (like the owner) had good reason to be frustrated with the fruitless tree, so the Lord Jesus Christ sees no good in us to persuade Him to be patient and kind towards us. He is well pictured by the keeper, who cared for the useless tree out of mercy and kindness alone.

Two courses of action. The expert vineyard-keeper suggested two courses of action: (1) to dig around the tree, and (2) to put in fertilizer. It was possible that when he dug around the roots of the tree he might find an infestation of worms or other harmful insects which were preventing the tree from developing and bearing fruit. Equally he would loosen any tight soil which was choking the tree, and so enable the roots to grow better. Also, the tree clearly needed further nutrients which would improve its health and make it strong and fruitful. Compare these negative and positive remedies with the kind of remedies which are necessary for the problem of *our* sinfulness and uselessness to God.

(1) **An infestation must be destroyed.** Is there still an 'infestation' or love of sin below the surface, deep in our hearts? Do we half want to follow Christ, but still love our sins *more*? Are we unwilling to give up some sin which we know is wrong? Urge the children to see the folly of this, and not to imagine that church attendance and sympathy with the Gospel is enough. Plead with them to go urgently to the Lord and pray for a cure for their love of sin. Turn them to the cross where they will see what their sin cost the Saviour.

(2) **Rich nutrients may be needed.** Equally, they may need further supplies of the Lord's message of redeeming grace. They may need the strong encouragements of the Gospel — a further view of how the Lord in His great love suffered every pang of punishment for the sin of His people. Even as He suffered He could see in His mind all those whose pardon He was securing (*Isaiah 53.10-11*).

Perhaps they need to see again the great life-changing character of conversion which we have described before, so that they may desire and pray for it. Here too we may supply the encouragement of testimony — either our own, or that of a notable Christian.

The warning. Explain that one thing is certain: God will not continue to overlook fruitlessness for ever. He would be unwise and unfair to do so. His patience must come to an end one day. He will then say, *What more was there to do . . . that I have not done . . . ? (Isaiah 5.4.)* God the Father has shown patience with us; God the Son has shown incomparable kindness and paid an infinite price to help us; God the Holy Spirit has shown us the remedy — the Gospel. But if we continue as souls useless to God, He will have no alternative but to remove us far from this life, and banish us from the glories of Heaven. Convey your concern to the class that any one of them should fall into this judgement.

Visual Aid

Teachers will find many helpful illustrations of fruit-trees (fruitful and diseased) in the mass of gardening books and magazines readily available. Those with gardens could provide samples of branches, fruit, packets of fertilizer, etc.

Revision (82)

Aim: This lesson review gives teachers an especially good opportunity to 'watch over' the souls given into their care (*Hebrews 13.17*).

The Lord's 'shock tactics'. In drawing together these parables and their meanings even the younger children will delight to notice how the Lord deliberately surprised His audiences. The person who turned out to be the 'hero' was never the person they expected. The rich, proud and 'religious' people ended up condemned, while the poor, despised sinners were forgiven and welcomed into Heaven. These points may be re-emphasised and demonstrated in the context of the whole series for older classes, who may smugly imagine that they know the parables very well. Help such children to put themselves in the place of the Lord's hearers who heard these parables for the first time and who did not expect that the rich businessman would be called a fool, or that the father would deal so kindly with the prodigal son, or that the tax-gatherer would be blessed by God rather than the Pharisee.

The often unnoticed surprises of the parables will help to maintain interest and challenge the children's attitudes and assumptions. The impact of surprise will help them to see if they resemble any of the foolish or deluded characters of the parables.

We should tell class members who are believers that the Lord often tested the sincerity of the 'professing believers' of the Jewish church by their attitude to the lost (as in *Luke 15*). Do they share His concern for the unsaved? Do they try to witness to unconverted friends at school, or do they pray for them?

Heaven and hell. Another unnoticed aspect of the parables which should be highlighted (briefly) is the teaching of the Lord in many of these parables about our ultimate destination.

If you have reason to believe that children in your class have been told that God welcomes everyone (forgiven or not) into Heaven, and He would never condemn anyone to hell, then turn them to the close of those parables which clearly show the opposite to be the case. Remind the children that most of these parables deal with final consequences; ultimate destinations; everlastingly fixed situations.

Revision questions. The following questions will form a basis for the lesson:

(1) We learned about a rich farmer. How did he become so rich? Why did God call him a fool?

(2) What happened when the lost coin and the lost sheep were found? Who is lost to God? How would you describe 'lost' people? What happens in Heaven when a sinner repents?

(3) Who took his father's wealth, went off to a distant country and wasted it away on pleasure? What did he decide to do when the money was all spent and he was starving? What surprise did he receive long before he reached home? What should we do when we realise what poor, hopeless sinners we are? What will God do if we return 'home'? What makes true Christians very happy?

(4) List some of the excuses received by the man who hosted a great feast. What excuses do people give for not accepting an invitation to church or Sunday School? What happens when people refuse God's kind invitation?

(5) Why did an injured Jew expect no kindness from a Samaritan? Of Whom was that Samaritan a picture? What did the Saviour pay for us to be healed and restored?

(6) What is hell like? What is Heaven like? How does God warn people of the dangers awaiting them? What kind of people will be carried to Heaven by angels when they die?

(7) Why did God not hear the prayer of the proud Pharisee? Why did He listen to the tax-gatherer? How did the Pharisee convince himself that he was a good man?

(8) What happened while the nobleman went away to be made a king? Why do so many people rebel against God? What does the money (which was given to the nobleman's servants) stand for? How must we invest (or trade with) the message of the Gospel? What will happen to us if we do this? And what will happen if we do not?

(9) Why did the owner of the vineyard want to cut down his fig-tree? Who asked him to spare it for one more year, and what did that person want to do to rescue the tree? What does the Lord God expect and deserve to see in our lives? What did the Saviour do so that we might be given another opportunity? What will happen to those people who refuse the help of the Lord?

Series 11
Joshua – 1 Samuel
JUDGEMENT AND DELIVERANCE

83 – Rahab Weighs the Evidence
Only one person (and her family) escaped when God judged the evil city of Jericho. What led to her deliverance? How did she escape with her life and her family as the city walls came crashing down around them? On the day of judgement will it be possible for us to escape? The book of *Hebrews* answers our questions with the words – BY FAITH *Rahab the harlot did not perish*.

84 – Achan Hides his Sin
Achan thought that he could get away with hiding his sin. But God saw. Soon his companions had to suffer the effects of his sin, and later he also was called to account. In a world where we grow accustomed to lies, evasion and excuses we must not allow ourselves to think that we can hide our sins from God, Who sees all.

85 – Gideon Serves the Lord
Despite warnings, in their new land the people of Israel became fascinated by the gods of Baal, which were 'blind' to their sin. At first they enjoyed the freedom to sin which their adopted 'worship' gave them, but soon they felt the sting. Would God come to their rescue? Would He forgive their unfaithfulness? Will He forgive us our sins?

86 – The Victory Over the Midianites

Hordes of Midianites with their countless camels prepared for battle against the Lord's people. Yet God reduced the Israelite army to a mere three hundred men. Then, when their victory came, it was clear that it was the Lord's doing. As we face the enemies of sin and death and hell we too must say, 'Thou must save, and Thou alone.'

87 – Laish: A Dream World

The people living in this idyllic valley closed their eyes to reality and pretended they had no enemies. It is easy to see how foolish they were. But are we being just as foolish?

88 – Ruth Finds a New Home

A young widow deserts her people, her religion, and her prospects in order to travel with her bereaved mother-in-law! She seeks shelter under the Lord's wings and becomes a member of the family of God. Similar surprises are possible for all who forsake this world and follow the Saviour.

89 – Samuel Hears God's Call

A young boy hears God's call. How is that call heard today? What does Samuel's response teach us?

90 – The People Demand a King

The people of Israel had enjoyed free, fair and successful government for many years, as long as they obeyed the Lord. Now they demand a king. The reason? They must be like the other countries around them. Are we also ruled by what others do?

91 – The Rise and Fall of a Proud King

Samuel arrives at the field of battle only to discover King Saul offering a sacrifice – the sacred work of a priest. Power has gone to his head and so the Lord rejects him, and matters go from bad to worse. Do we realise that being proud will lead to an eternal fall?

92 – Revision

The outcome of all the events and the destiny of all the characters in this series of lessons hinge on whether or not faith in God was exercised. Thousands of years have passed since the days of Joshua, the Judges and Saul, but believing in God is still all that really matters.

Rahab Weighs the Evidence (83)

Joshua 2 and 6 (especially 6.1 and 22-25); Hebrews 11.31

Aim: To show how Rahab, though an 'outsider', came to appreciate the facts about God. To urge the children to follow Rahab's example and find a way of escape from God's judgement of sin.

Lesson Outline

Invite your class to imagine Rahab's unusual house, built in the tall, sturdy walls of the city of Jericho. From her vantage-point Rahab could well imagine the horrors of a siege, and news that the Israelites were moving closer to Canaan every day was constantly being received in Jericho.

The likelihood of death troubled her. This news also worried Rahab because it pricked her conscience. She had lived a sinful life and done anything which would bring her money. The whole city was in rebellion against the true God and filled with people who wanted to sin as much as they liked. There were no churches in Jericho where the true God was worshipped, only idol-temples and the equivalent of night-clubs, pubs and brothels. The pathetic, little carvings which they called their gods were only a licence for sin. Evening 'worship' of these deities was a thinly disguised excuse for drunken parties. Cheating, lying, cruelty and immorality were commonplace, and people were out to get all they could for themselves.

Rahab trembled as she thought of the advancing army of Israelites because her conscience told her that she deserved to have trouble come upon her. News travelled quite efficiently in those days (despite the lack of modern communications) and over the years Rahab had heard much about the people of Israel and their God. From all this news she had come to understand the following things about the true God:—

(1) He is a God of power. Rahab had heard reports of what the Lord had done for the Israelites; how He had opened the Red Sea as a way of escape from the mighty Egyptians, and how He had destroyed every enemy who tried to stop them in their journey. She had concluded that He was the one true God — the *God in heaven above and on earth beneath (Joshua 2.11)*. She realised that the walls of Jericho offered her no protection from such a mighty God.

(2) **He is a holy God.** Rahab had also received reports that the Hebrews' God was a righteous God, not a god who encouraged sin, like the man-made gods and goddesses of Canaan. The Israelites' God expected His people to be holy. He gave laws against sin. People who killed, stole, committed adultery or blasphemed were severely punished, and everyone was taught to live a life which pleased Him by caring for others more than themselves. The Israelites did not offer sacrifices in the way that the Canaanites did, bribing their gods for favours. Israelite sacrifices were offered with heartfelt sorrow for sin. They did not achieve anything, for they were designed solely to teach a message. They signified that sin must be punished, and that one day God would have to provide a costly sacrifice to pay the price of sin.

Rahab faced the facts. Let the children imagine Rahab standing at her window looking across the plains, expecting any day to see signs of the Israelites approaching. Other people in Jericho were frightened at the news but decided nothing could be done. They liked to think that the city walls would offer them protection, and in the meantime they went on enjoying their sins and drowning their fears with renewed excursions into sinful pleasures.

But Rahab was different. She faced the facts. Instead of pushing fear to one side, she began to prepare for what must soon come to pass. How could she be ready to meet such a mighty and holy God? Remind the class that our days too are numbered. How can we prepare for that great day when our physical existence ends, and we have to face the Lord?

Rahab repented. Rahab realised that she would have to leave her old, sinful life and pray to the God of Israel for forgiveness. From now on she would have to earn her living honestly. Soon she was to be found laying out flax on her roof — an indication of her new occupation. Show the children that for each one of us repentance is a very practical matter. It means leaving our sins and asking God to change our lives.

Rahab renounced her old citizenship. Describe how the spies, with immense courage, entered into Jericho, but were quickly detected and reported to the king. When the moment came that the Israelite spies knocked at her door, Rahab knew that she must take a stand. She must either remain a loyal member of Jericho, or she must give a safe haven to the Israelites. If she changed sides and protected the spies she would be running the risk of discovery and execution. All this must have passed through her mind, but she was ready to take her stand for the Lord, and she invited the spies in.

Tell the children that when we come to understand the message of the Gospel, we realise that repentance involves changing from one side to another. The moment will come at home or at school when we shall be faced with a question of allegiance — are we on the world's side or the Lord's? Like Rahab we must be prepared to stand for the Lord no matter what the cost. We must be willing to obey Him, and to do His will.

Rahab trusted. What enabled Rahab to take her stand? It was the fact that she believed in the Lord and was convinced that He would save her. With this conviction she asked the spies to spare her when the day of battle came, and she welcomed their suggestion that she should hang the scarlet cord from her window to mark out her home from the rest of the city. Even though she had never met these Israelites before, she trusted them when they promised that her life would be spared.

Show the class that above all else God desires that we trust Him and His message. When we hear from our Sunday School teachers that, despite our sin, God is willing to forgive us, and that He sent His own dear Son to bear the pain and penalty for every offence we have committed, then we must believe God's Word and put our future and our total trust in His promise. Just as Rahab's life hung on that scarlet cord, so our eternal future rests on the Lord Jesus and what He did for us on Calvary.

Rahab was delivered. Tell how the Israelites marched around Jericho, and how the inhabitants, puzzled and fearful, watched the sequence of events. Describe briefly the marching round the walls. As the fear of the people increased they heard the sound of the trumpets of rams' horns followed by the great shout and the terrible din of the cracking and crumbling of the mighty walls. Compare this with the last day of an unbeliever. For many years he fears death, and then the moment comes when all that he trusted in during this life crumbles away and he wakes up in another world, having left the world in which he had the opportunity to repent.

In Jericho, Rahab watched with anticipation. For her it seemed like a rescue operation. Soon she would be away from the stench of that evil city which had so nearly claimed her as a victim. Soon she would be 'at home' among the Lord's people. Can you look forward to that great day at the end of this world's history, when the Lord Jesus will return to judge all evil and to take His people to be with Him for ever?

Achan Hides his Sin (84)

Joshua 6.17-19; 7.1-26

Aim: To show that God cannot be deceived, and that sin has costly consequences both in this life and eternally.

Lesson Outline

Suggest that many children do not take Sunday School lessons seriously or turn to the Saviour because they do not have enough respect or reverence either for the Lord or for His day of judgement. Even though they vaguely realise that God exists, they imagine that somehow He does not know about their sin, and that He will never deal with it. This lesson tells us about a man who took this very attitude.

Forbidden treasure. Explain that when the Lord gave the Israelites instructions for the taking of the evil city of Jericho, He commanded that all valuables were to be placed in the treasury of the Lord, and that the Israelite soldiers were not to sift through the ruins of the city in case they should be tempted to loot the valuable goods lying around. The warning was clearly given that if anyone took things for himself he would bring trouble upon the whole Israelite camp.

Achan is tempted. Describe how Achan disobeyed the Lord. Instead of rejoicing in the victory, Achan began to turn over the rubble. Soon he spotted a beautiful garment, made in Babylon, together with silver and gold of great value. As he gazed at these valuables he felt an irresistible urge to have them. It may be that he resisted these temptations at first, but the more he looked, the more determined he became to take these things, convincing himself that no one need ever know. Among the things which Achan took, the bar of gold alone would have been worth a fortune. He had to stay up late secretly digging a hole in the earth under his tent to hide his treasure. Imagine how he must have lied to deceive his friends and neighbours to explain his mysterious activities.

Picture Achan's frustration as he began to realise that these goods, for which he was probably already paying dearly in terms of a guilty conscience, were really rather useless to him. When would he wear the beautiful, gold-threaded robe? As soon as he put it on, it would be obvious to all that he had committed a great sin. Where would he spend the gold, and how would he explain where it came from? One day, surely, the truth was bound to come out. But Achan shrugged off these problems, thinking that one day his secret treasure would bring him great benefits.

No secrets from God. Remind the class that no one can keep secrets from God. He knows all and sees all. He even reads our thoughts and knows our motives. Achan had buried his treasure safely away from human gaze, but God had watched everything he had done, and soon some surprising events began to occur.

(a) Defeat at Ai. Help the class to imagine the shock and the humiliation felt by the people of Israel as news reached them that their army had been routed and put to flight at Ai. After witnessing so many miracles from the Lord on their behalf, and after seeing the walls of Jericho collapse in a heap before them, the people were puzzled and very distressed to hear how the battle for such a comparatively small city had been lost. Joshua and the elders were distraught, and prayed to the Lord to find out why He had withdrawn His power from them. The explanation was simple. There was a case of deliberate sin in the camp.

(b) A remedy. God's remedy was clear. The offender must be found and punished. Describe the solemn scene as Joshua gathered the tribes one by one, until he discovered the one to which the offender belonged. (Describe the process so as to rivet the attention of the class.) The search then narrowed to one family, and finally Achan was confronted. What had he taken? What had he done which so grieved and angered the Lord?

Gaining and losing. Achan now saw how foolish he had been. He had gained some valuables, but he had lost things which were far more valuable – the favour and blessing of God, and his life also. How he must have regretted that moment when the beautiful mantle from Babylon dazzled him. Remind the children of the words of the Lord Jesus Christ when He warned, *Whoever wishes to save his life shall lose it . . . For what does it profit a man to gain the whole world, and forfeit his soul? (Mark 8.35-36.)* Describe the tragedy of young people who, for the sake of temporary pleasures, put their eternal future in jeopardy.

A Gospel conclusion. Remind the class of Achan's casual approach to sin. He took the treasure, buried it and shrugged his shoulders. Only later did the Lord make him face up to the true ugliness and implications of his act. Look at the Lord's diagnosis of his sin *(Joshua 7.11)* and its parallels with ours: –

(a) **'You have taken!'** Achan had committed a deliberate and wilful act of disobedience against God's clear command. Remind the class that all sin has this ugly dimension. We do not just *happen* to steal or lie or cheat. In all our sin we deliberately defy the Lord our Maker and flout His laws.

(b) **'You have stolen!'** These treasures were not Achan's to take. God had given a remarkable victory, and many Israelites had joined in the conquest. Who was Achan to think that he had the right to help himself to the valuables which others left alone? Again this provides an illustration of our sin. When we choose to go our own way and dismiss the Lord from our lives, who do we think we are? Who gave us our minds and bodies? Who made the world and everything in it? What right do we think we have to steal our lives from God?

(c) **'You have deceived!'** Achan had to hide his ill-gotten gain. He had to live a lie! He became sneaking and devious. Help the children to see that sin always has this effect. So much sin involves lying, cheating, and covering up with excuses. We deceive ourselves, we deceive others and we try to deceive God. We tell ourselves that we have done nothing really wrong, or that it was not our fault, or that it will not harm anyone else, etc. The more we sin, the more we warp our sense of right and wrong, and the more cunning we become as liars.

The consequences. One day Achan had to face the fact that his action had cost the lives of thirty-six others, brought shame to his nation and cost him and his family their lives. If we cover up our sin and never repent, we shall one day be summoned before God for judgement, and then we shall see (too late) the seriousness and the consequences of all our sin. Sin is never trivial. It is vile and costly. Because the Saviour saw the enormity of our sin and its tragic cost, He was willing to come and give His life so that we might be rescued from its clutches. Have you ever faced up to the vileness and nastiness of sin? Have you seen how desperately you need a Saviour to rescue you from its guilt and power? Have you learned to appreciate the kindness of the Saviour in giving His life? Achan was severely punished, and this incident is recorded in God's Word so that we might learn, and seek the Saviour while He still stands ready to receive us.

Visual Aid

A simple picture of the inside of a tent with an openable flap to the floor will provide a fascinating presentation for younger classes. At the appropriate point in the lesson open the flap and hide Achan's treasure. Write out the three accusations clearly on separate pieces of card: — You have taken! You have stolen! You have deceived!

In a different colour and in capitals write on a larger piece of card: — YOU NEED A SAVIOUR!

Gideon Serves the Lord (85)

Joshua 23; Judges 6.1-32

Aim: To teach that God is full of mercy, and willing to save us from our rebellion against Him, but like Gideon we must be willing to destroy the other 'gods' which we have put in His place.

Lesson Outline

Tell how the Israelites had gradually moved into the land of Canaan and conquered it. The Canaanites were so evil that God punished them and gave their land to the Israelites, who conquered them at His specific command. Details are given in the book of *Joshua*, where we read of Joshua's faithfulness and of the success which the Lord granted him (*Joshua 11.23*). Picture the many tribes and families settling in the areas allocated to them, cultivating their lands, building homes and enjoying a period of rest and prosperity (*Joshua 23.1*). Read or summarise Joshua's parting speech:

(a) He attributed all their success to the Lord Who had fought for them (*Joshua 23.3*).

(b) He urged and commanded them to obey God's laws meticulously (v 6).

(c) He forbade them to serve or bow down to other gods, warning them of the dire consequences (v 16).

Warnings ignored. Explain that as time passed, the generation involved in these battles died out, and the next generation took all their blessings for granted, forgetting what the Lord had done for their nation. Worse still, they began to worship the pathetic and perverted idol-gods of the Canaanites. Imagine younger people becoming bored with listening to the wonderful accounts of how God had repeatedly intervened to give victories to their grandparents. Before long, young men and women who had been brought up to reverence the Lord and obey His great commandments, were to be seen dancing in drunken orgies around the Baal images, and bowing down to gods which allowed them to indulge freely in all kinds of sin.

The consequences. Soon they discovered what God thought of them. Instead of helping them, He stopped protecting them and allowed their enemies to overpower them (*Judges 2.14-23*). Describe the state of affairs which prevailed when Gideon was a young man (*Judges 6.1-6*). The Israelites had been reduced to a poor, humiliated people whose hard-earned products were quickly and ruthlessly plundered by the Midianites. Describe how an entire family would till the land, plant the seed, weed and water, and finally harvest the crop, only to have it taken overnight, leaving them with little or no food for the winter. This had gone on for seven years.

Where sin leads us. Show how this illustrates very well the consequences of sinning against God in our own day. Sin seems to offer people a happy life, but really it steals from them everything which is really worth having. *The wages of sin is death (Romans 6.23)*. People are tempted to believe that sin (bending the truth, doing others down, misusing bodily pleasures, living for greedy, selfish gain, etc) will make them happy, but sooner or later they discover that sin has had the following effects:-

(a) They have been made *poor*. Sin not only robs them of their money, but also of peace of mind, and a place in Heaven.

(b) They have been *humiliated*. Just as the great nation of Israel became a weak and pathetic laughing-stock among its neighbours, so sin weakens people. It takes away integrity, self-control, kindness and other strengths, making them ugly in the sight of a holy God.

(c) They have been *separated from their God and Saviour*, Who alone can bless and help people. They have become like the prodigal son in a far country, far away from any experience of the goodness and power of God.

What can be done? Eventually these Israelites began to cry to the Lord for help as they saw their farms raided and their peace shattered (*Judges 6.6*). Although they deserved nothing from God, yet He heard their prayers, and soon He appointed a young man named Gideon to be their deliverer. Remind the class that when we come to our senses and see how wrong it is to rebel against the Lord, we too can cry out to Him for His forgiveness. Already He has sent a Deliverer, a Saviour, Who was willing to suffer the terrible consequences of our waywardness to set us free from sin.

First instructions. Before Gideon could engage the Midianites in battle and deal with their cruel tyranny, there was an important matter to be dealt with. Before God could give His blessing or save Israel, Baal had to be destroyed. Remind children that the same principle holds good with us. How can we ask God to forgive our past sins if we deliberately, secretly intend to hold on to many of them? When we seek forgiveness, we must be willing to give up those things which have taken the place of God in our lives. Explain that this action was not easy for Gideon. He would meet strong opposition.

Threats and fears. Most of the people who lived in Gideon's village had a superstitious regard for Baal. They thought that terrible things would happen to them if anyone dared to destroy his image. No doubt Satan sought to intimidate Gideon with fears of angering the people. What would the villagers do when they discovered their Baal statue cut to pieces? Tell the children that it is never easy to leave the wide road which the crowd takes, and to seek the Lord. They may be afraid of what friends will think of them. The Lord Jesus Christ warned that if we follow Him we may well meet with scorn and hostility from even our family and friends. Teachers of older classes can give examples known to them of this kind of intimidation. We may be frightened that we shall be laughed at, or that we will lose some of our pleasures.

Replaced by joyful zeal. Despite these dire threats and fears, Gideon could not be put off. Conclude the lesson with an exciting account of how he and his servants set out at dead of night to tear down the altar of Baal and replace it with an altar to the Lord. Any fear was completely overcome by a desire to get rid of this false god. Gideon took delight in destroying this manifestation of a religion which had stolen the hearts of God's people and taught them to sin so grievously that they had gone away from the Lord and His blessings.

Explain to the class that when we are converted by the Lord our fears will also be banished. Suddenly, instead of worrying about the cost of following the Saviour, we shall be filled with a sense of wonder and amazement that He should ever give us the privilege of being His disciples. As the Holy Spirit opens our eyes, we too shall see how deceitful and empty the gods of this world are.

The great test. The children will enjoy hearing about the events of the following morning when an inquest was held by the men of the city. Gideon could not escape suspicion for long, and soon his father's front door was surrounded by an angry mob demanding his death. Close the lesson with his father's wise words — *If he is a god, let him contend for himself* (v 31). This advice was accepted.

You may ask the class, 'What happened to Gideon?' When

they reply that nothing happened, you will be able to press home to them the powerlessness of worldly gods. Urge them not to entrust their lives to activities, interests or possessions which will take them away from the Lord. Instead point them to the Saviour – the God Who made Heaven and earth, and Who withstood the powers of death and hell when He died on Calvary's cross for His people. Help them to see the wonder of the fact that such a mighty God should love such people as them and call them to Himself.

The Victory Over the Midianites (86)

Judges 7

Aim: To teach how the Lord showed the Israelites that He alone could deliver them from the mighty Midianites, and to show that the Lord alone can save *us* from our *spiritual* enemies.

Lesson Outline

Remind the class of the trouble the Israelites were in. Because they had been unfaithful to the Lord, they had been left unprotected and unhelped by Him. The new gods which they worshipped were lifeless idols which could not help them. The people had been humiliated and made desperately poor by the enemy, having become virtually a nation of slaves, producing crops and herds for the enemy to plunder at will.

The Midianite threat. Now a great company of Midianites and others were encamped just to the north of their territory – *as numerous as locusts; and their camels were without number, as numerous as the sand on the seashore (Judges 7.12).* How could the Jews, a demoralised and frightened people, hope to overcome such a vast and experienced enemy? Remind the children of how the Lord had found one young man who was willing to destroy Baal and to worship the one true God. The Lord now planned to use Gideon to answer the prayers of His people for deliverance from the Midianites. They had no hope whatsoever of saving themselves, but now that they had seen the folly of their ways and returned to the Lord, it was possible that He would be God's 'saviour' to lead them.

Our enemy. Explain that we also have a great enemy, the

devil. Because we cannot see him, we are tempted to believe he does not exist. This does not alter the fact that he is there, but it does make his attacks more deadly. No army will defend itself if it does not believe the enemy exists. A picture of the Midianite camp with its many tents could be used to illustrate the spiritual enemies we all face. At the centre, place a large tent belonging to the devil. His aim is to keep us under his control until the day of judgement when he will triumphantly claim us as his own. Not until he sees us finally in hell will he turn his back on us.

Around this central tent, picture the tents of ten great 'regiments' of sin (listed in the ten commandments) employed in the devil's army. These are Satan's many temptations. As archers shoot arrows at their victims, so temptations are shot into our minds — temptations such as anger, hatred, envy, jealousy, lying, cheating, boasting, and so on. Some of Satan's archers shoot arrows of greed and selfish desire into our hearts, so that we constantly want to have things that we see. Each temptation is intended to make us increasingly sinful, and also increasingly helpless in the clutches of the devil. Like the Israelites of old we need to realise how strong our enemy is and how weak we are. We need to long to escape and find freedom from the devil's tyranny. Only if we cry to the Lord to come to our rescue do we have any hope. He alone can deal with Satan for us.

Gideon's army. Return to the biblical narrative and tell how an army of 32,000 men gathered under Gideon. As they lined up they must have seemed quite a large force, but in fact they were quite tiny in comparison to the Midianite army. However, the Lord was not prepared to bless them if, after gaining the victory, they would quickly forget what He had done for them, and begin to boast, saying, 'Our own power has saved us!' Therefore God ordered a great reduction in the numbers and Gideon sent home any man who was fearful or reluctant to fight. Only 10,000 remained. Warn the children of the fatal self-confidence which causes people to imagine that they are capable of defeating temptations and overcoming their sinful tendencies by themselves. God will not set us free from the power of sin and of Satan until we realise that we *depend entirely* on His power to change our lives.

Go on to explain how the army was finally reduced to a mere

300 men. These men were not picked because they were extra strong warriors. They were those who did not kneel down to drink water at a stream. Why was this? Some people think that it was because they were alert and vigilant people. But the most likely reason is that the idol-worshippers kneeled before Baal, and these 300 men were faithful Israelites who could not bring themselves to kneel, and thus resemble idolaters. So, the army was whittled down to a faithful few. We know that these men did not subsequently criticise Gideon's strange instructions, but they trusted their lives and the outcome of the battle to the Lord. Before long they experienced the joy of a very great victory. Explain that the Lord is willing to save all those who humbly obey Him and accept His way of salvation.

The night of battle. Illustrate the Lord's kindness in helping us to overcome our doubts and fears. We may wonder within ourselves, 'Could *I* ever be saved and become a Christian?' The Lord knows our fears. He knew Gideon's fears and so He sent him down to the Midianite camp where he overheard the man's strange dream (*Judges 7.13-14*) − a signal to Gideon that the Lord was already at work preparing the way. He returned confidently to his 300 men to issue their instructions.

Describe the exciting course of the night's events. Three units of a hundred men each were soon stationed around the enemy camp, bearing their empty pitchers (earthenware containers for food or drink) which covered flaming torches. In their other hand they held their trumpets. Let the children enjoy imagining the scene. As Gideon gave the word, the pitchers were smashed, the torches raised and in unison the great battle cry went up − *A sword for the Lord and for Gideon!*

Terror struck into the Midianite army and before long utter confusion had broken loose in their camp. Soon they were fleeing for their lives. Their proud, aggressive princes were captured and destroyed, and the people of Israel at last could live safely in the comfort of their own homes. The Lord had won a great victory. None of the 300 claimed the glory for themselves. Of course, even had they tried to do so, it would have seemed ridiculous to everyone because it was obvious that only the Lord could have brought about such a result, and so give victory to a mightily outnumbered force.

Our Deliverer. Close the lesson by showing how the Lord

Jesus Christ came to do battle with Satan on our behalf. Remind the class that He became a man (God and man), and lived on this earth a life of absolute sinlessness and perfection. Then He went to the cross of Calvary to bear the terrible punishment which sinners deserve for all their sin. In taking this punishment, He paid the price on behalf of all who seek His help, and set them free from the dominion and power of Satan. We cannot get rid of Satan's control or change our lives ourselves, but the Lord can.

The Israelites had to fight their enemy in the way God said. They had to reduce the number of their soldiers, and simply trust the instructions which God gave them. So today, to be set free from Satan's control, and to become real Christians, we must stop thinking that we can do anything to win this victory by ourselves.

No matter how 'big' our army (in other words, no matter how much effort we make) we can neither cure our sinful hearts, nor resist temptation successfully, nor can we by our own will-power find the Lord Jesus and come to know Him, nor can we by our own efforts earn a place in Heaven. We must abandon that kind of thinking, and simply follow the instructions which the Lord gives. The Israelites were told exactly what to do — and so are we.

To be delivered from the devil and all his temptations, we must go in prayer to the Lord Jesus Christ. We must sincerely repent of our sin and implore His mercy and forgiveness. We must very definitely put our trust in what He has done on Calvary's cross in taking the punishment in our place, and thank Him for His amazing love. And we must give Him our lives, asking Him to change us and make Himself known to us. If (like Gideon and his men) we follow God's instructions with all our hearts, we shall have an amazing experience. We shall be made true Christians, set free from Satan's control, and we shall know that we are different people.

Laish: A Dream World (87)

Judges 18 (especially verses 7-11 and 27-29)

Aim: To warn the children against living in a fool's paradise with their eyes closed to the vital issues of life and eternity.

Lesson Outline

Describe the picturesque valley close to the slopes of Mount Hermon where the people of Laish lived. It could best be compared with the kind of Swiss alpine scene so often featured in calendars, except that the climate was warmer and the vegetation richer. On the slopes of the mountains grew the world-renowned cedars of Lebanon with their massive trunks and unusual flat, evergreen branches. Today the region is in south-west Lebanon, and is linked with the port of Sidon by a pipeline carrying oil from Iran. The link between Laish and Sidon is very ancient. Some years before the events of our lesson Sidon was a great Phoenician trading port. It was flanked by mountains and depended on the inland valley district of Laish for all its food supplies, as well as for timber. The Sidonians had invested enormous effort and money to build a road across the mountain range and to develop the rich land and woods of Laish as a food production centre.

But then the city of Sidon was besieged and destroyed by enemies, and the remote, isolated town of Laish ended up with marvellous facilities for farming and industry, and no 'master' to serve. Suddenly they had all their resources to themselves! They revelled in their unexpected independence and liberty, enjoying to the full this secluded region — *where there is no lack of anything that is on the earth.*

Let the children picture this haven of prosperity. There was plenty of land and goods to go round. Every family enjoyed a spacious home with many luxuries and rich food. However, the people of Laish very quickly took their benefits for granted and became utterly selfish. The Bible tells us that spies sent from the tribe of Dan to survey the land discovered them to be — *careless . . . quiet and secure; and there was no magistrate in the land* (*AV*). Examine each word in turn. Four word-cards will focus attention. (For the information of teachers, the Danite's search for new territory took place long after the conquest and the death of Joshua, at the very end of the period of the Judges.)

(1) Careless. (Without cares.) Living in this little paradise the people of Laish gave themselves over to the pleasures and prosperity which surrounded them. They did not want to be bothered with questions such as, 'What is life for?' or, 'Should we be helping anyone else in this world?' or, 'What if some unexpected disaster were to strike?' They had no interest in such problems. They became utterly complacent. Their own selfish and immediate comforts were their only concern.

(2) **Quiet.** Because they were so amply provided for, they needed to put little effort into life. They could afford to ignore trading with other cities and concentrate on their own pleasures. They took no interest in anyone but themselves.

(3) **Secure.** They saw no need for alliances or help from stronger neighbours, and trusted in their own isolation (v 28). It never occurred to them that they could ever be in danger of attack from an enemy. They had done away with the expense of an army. Their young men did not want the restrictions of military service, and so the people remained completely unprotected.

(4) **No ruler or magistrate.** They even did away with magistrates or rulers, so that they could claim to be a totally free society with no one to enforce law and order. If they did wrong they did not want to face up to the consequences. Having abolished their 'police force' they could do just as they liked. They hated rules, and did not want their lives to be governed by anyone.

But what happened to Laish? Describe how the spy party from the tribe of Dan was sent out to search for new territory, and how they came across this amazingly fertile valley and decided it was an ideal place for their large community of people to come and settle in. Describe also their astonishment at finding the region so unguarded and the inhabitants so naive. The spies returned home, and very soon a force of only six hundred soldiers was despatched to Laish. Yet this small body of troops was quite enough to overpower the people and burn their city. Never before had a territory been invaded so easily. Soon the area was renamed Dan, and the city of Laish was forgotten, except that the Lord God recorded this incident in His Word so that we might learn from it. Using the same word-cards show how easy it is for us to behave just like the people of Laish, especially in our attitude to God and to spiritual dangers. (Teachers will need to expand on the following headings, according to the age of their children.)

(1) Careless. We too do not want to be troubled with worries about the state of our character or the future of our souls. We do not want to grow up when it comes to facing the real issues of life. We have a tendency to hide away from the unpleasant things of life. Why is the subject of death not spoken about by people very much? We tend to gamble on the fact that somehow everything will turn out all right. We will trust 'luck' rather than seek help and guidance and protection from the Lord, Who alone provides for the real needs of people.

(2) Quiet. We make no attempt to be of service to God or to other people. We become very selfish — busy getting what we want, having fun, and pleasing ourselves. Anything which does not please us we ignore.

(3) Secure. We do not realise that we have big enemies in life: Satan, who aims to trap us in a life of sin and unbelief; and the false ideas of many people which take us far away from God and from real happiness. We imagine we are safe and secure when in fact we are vulnerable, and such easy prey. We leave ourselves wide open to the attacks of Satan, to evil and the troubles of life. The weakest person is the one who does not expect to be attacked!

(4) No ruler or magistrate. Many of us take one look at God's law and decide we do not want it. We want to be free, to have our own way and to leave God out of our lives.

Remind the children that in one day the people of Laish lost everything: their lives, their homes, their country. What a terrible humiliation for these proud, wealthy people — especially their strong, well-fed young men — to find themselves attacked and overpowered so easily by the swordsmen and archers of the Danites. How they must have wished that they had a powerful neighbour who would come to their rescue.

Urge the children to face the fact that they too have enemies. Sin is an enemy. Satan wants to have them in his power. Misfortunes and tragedies will hurt them. Illnesses will infect them. Finally, death waits to strike. They cannot afford to lead a life independent of God. They need a deliverer, the Saviour, Who will help them face and conquer these foes.

Ruth Finds a New Home (88)

Ruth; see also Leviticus 19.9-10; Deuteronomy 25.5-10

Aim: To use the message of Ruth as a demonstration of how all needy sinners should approach their Redeemer, and find the blessings He bestows on all *who seek refuge under His wings.*

Lesson Outline

Picture the sad scene near the border crossing post of Moab and Israel. A middle-aged woman, Naomi, her face bearing the strain of sorrow and grief, yet composed and kind, urges her two daughters-in-law to turn back to their homes and families, wishing them God's blessing. Both of the young women are weeping. Neither of them wants to leave her mother-in-law. Why?

A mother-in-law's testimony. Explain the trials and tragedies which had befallen Naomi, namely: —

(a) the difficulties she must have encountered as an immigrant in the land of Moab, where religion and culture were quite different from that of her own land;

(b) the death of her husband, followed shortly by —

(c) the death of her two sons.

Explain how Naomi's godly behaviour and demeanour must have deeply impressed the two young widows. They had noticed the contrast between the kind and godly Naomi and the selfish, worldly women of Moab. They had been able to observe her closely under very testing circumstances, as one bereavement followed another. They had seen how much she loved her family and also how much she trusted her God. Unlike the Moabites who worshipped idols and turned to superstitious remedies for grief, Naomi trusted the one true God Who made Heaven and earth.

Tell the class that many people have started to seek the Lord because of the testimony of a Christian friend or relative. When we see a person whose life is changed and different, we also ought to ask why. Orpah and Ruth were both impressed by Naomi's trust in God, but Ruth went a step further. She, herself, came to trust the Lord as her Saviour. We know this because of what happened next.

Orpah's response. Describe how Orpah and Ruth both expressed their desire to return with Naomi to her land and people. But then Naomi kindly and wisely explained the cost of such a step. She reminded them that in her land, as foreigners, they would have very little prospect of marriage. In those days marriage meant even more to a woman than it does today, for it was generally impossible for women to get jobs and support themselves as individuals. So she advised them to turn back. Orpah, sad at heart, agreed but Ruth refused. Why?

Ruth's response. Explain that by clinging to Naomi, Ruth would be cutting her ties with her home, her family, her people and her religion. Quote her memorable words from *Ruth 1.16-17*. Have these words printed out and encourage the class to learn them. It seemed likely that Ruth would face a life of poverty and loneliness (certainly once Naomi died), yet she was so anxious to live and worship with Naomi that she intreated her mother-in-law to let her go with her. Her respect and affection for Naomi had led her to seek Naomi's God, and having tasted His love and goodness she would not part from Him for all the world.

Our response. Remind the class of the words of the Lord Jesus, *If anyone wishes to come after Me, let him deny himself, and take up his cross, and follow Me (Mark 8.34)*. Once people have really found the Lord they are determined not to be parted from Him. Knowing Christ is a very real experience. Encourage your class to give priority to travelling through life with Christ as their Saviour.

Difficult days. Days of hardship followed. There was the long journey to Bethlehem, and when they reached the city there was a great stir. People hardly recognised Naomi. She looked so much older than when they had last seen her. And who was this foreign woman who travelled with her? To add to her trials Naomi had financial problems to worry about (see *Ruth 4.3*). Probably the two women found a simple little place in which to stay, and Ruth had to work hard to make it fit to live in. Next she had to find 'work', and set off early in the morning to glean in the barley fields.

God's rich provision. In chapter 2 we read that Ruth *HAPPENED to come to the portion of the field belonging to Boaz (a* rich relative of Naomi). Now that Ruth's life had been placed in the Lord's hands, she found that even everyday circumstances were under His care. Explain to the class how this event turned out to be so helpful. Instead of being ostracised as a foreigner, she was given special attention by Boaz and his servants. Her dedication to the Lord led to her being blessed, and able to gather ample barley and wheat to keep Naomi and herself for the future year.

How Ruth approached Boaz. Tell how Naomi then instructed Ruth in seeking even greater blessing. She was entitled to ask Boaz to act as her relative and 'redeemer'. The Lord God, in His law, had made provision for the unfortunate, like Ruth. Not only was she allowed to glean but she could ask her husband's brother to take her husband's place so that children could be raised and her husband's name be perpetuated (*Deuteronomy 25.5*). So it was that Ruth, a poor immigrant, tremblingly lay herself at Boaz's feet and claimed his covering and his care.

How we must approach the Lord. Suggest to the class that this is a picture for us of the seeker's approach to the Lord. We too are poor and needy. We have no goodness (no merit) of our own and no eternal home. Our debt of sin should be worrying us. We come from a people who have no time for God and who have made themselves His enemies. We, too, can only throw ourselves on His mercy, asking Him to cover us with the righteousness of the Lord Jesus, His Son, our Saviour.

'Ask, and it shall be given.' Ruth was not disappointed. The very next day Boaz made arrangements to settle Naomi's financial needs. Ruth was no longer obligated to pay the family debts, for Boaz had 'redeemed' her. Better still he agreed to marry her. Soon she moved into his house and before long she had the joy of nursing their little son Obed. Fill in the picture for your children. Assure them that the Lord answers our cries, just as Boaz did Ruth's. As soon as we cry out to God, really meaning our prayers, He pays off the debt of our sins and gathers us to Himself — *the way a hen gathers her chicks under her wings (Matthew 23.37)*.

A member of the royal family. The book of *Ruth* ends with even better news. Not only did the lonely young widow become a mother, richly provided for, but she was to be the great grandmother of the great King David — whose descendant was none other than the Lord Jesus Christ. She became, clearly, a member of *God's* family. Show the children that this will be their privilege too if they also turn for shelter under the righteousness of the Saviour. They will not only be forgiven and restored, but adopted into God's own dear family, becoming heirs together with the Lord Jesus.

Missing out. Think of poor Orpah! How much she missed by turning back to Moab and its false gods. Urge the children to follow the example of Ruth, and to trust their lives to the Saviour. The Lord has limitless blessings to bestow on all who forsake this world to follow Him, casting themselves on His lovingkindness and tender mercy.

Samuel Hears God's Call (89)

1 Samuel 2.35; 3

Aim: To so describe this childhood conversion that children will discover whether or not they have had such an experience. In particular, to explain that being a Christian involves *knowing* the Lord.

Lesson Outline

For older classes, open with some provocative questions to awaken interest in the lesson. Can young people and children be converted? What makes a person a Christian? Are all children brought up in church surroundings automatically Christians? How do we know if we are converted?

In the right place. Without going into the details of his birth, introduce the class to the young boy who lived and worked in the Tabernacle (called the Temple, but not of a permanent kind) in the city of Shiloh. From before his birth his mother had given him to the Lord's service. Samuel had been an answer to his mother's fervent prayers and at a young age she had brought him to Eli the priest, to work in the Tabernacle. We do not know Samuel's exact age at the time of his conversion. We only know that his mother had been delivering 'little robes' for several years and that he was still a boy (*1 Samuel 2.18-19* and *3.1*). Perhaps he was around the age of ten.

What kind of child had Samuel become? Did he grumble at being away from home — like a boy at boarding school? Was he curious to pry into the evil ways of Eli's sons, who so saddened their father? Did he allow the sordid atmosphere created by these two corrupt, immoral men to influence him? The glimpses we have into Samuel's everyday life suggest the opposite. We see him as a willing worker, ready at a moment's notice to spring to Eli's assistance. He did not yet know the Lord in a certain and direct way, but he was eager to be in the right place, and he greatly respected the Lord. Encourage the children in your class who cannot yet point to a conversion experience, but who are similarly seeking the Lord in an earnest way, never to be satisfied until they know they have found Him for themselves.

Knowing the Lord. One important job at the Tabernacle was to care for the copy of the Scriptures (the books written by Moses at God's bidding). Few people had the opportunity, as Samuel did, to handle those precious and special scrolls, and he cared for them most zealously. Yet, although Samuel valued and respected the Word of God, we are told that he did not yet know the Lord. He knew about the great things God had done for the Israelites, but he had never felt the nearness and power of God for himself.

Explain to the class that it is possible for them too to respect the Bible, bring a copy to Sunday School each week, learn passages by heart and even pass tests or exams in Bible knowledge, and yet not to have any personal experience of having come to know the Lord.

God's call by night. Describe the night when the young Samuel helped the old priest Eli, now almost blind, to his bed. Then it was Samuel's turn to lie down at the end of a busy day. We do not know whether Samuel had fallen asleep, or whether he lay thinking to himself — perhaps about his mother and father and their next visit to him. Suddenly Samuel clearly heard his name called twice, and he immediately assumed that it was Eli calling. Describe these events, up to the point that Eli perceived that it was God calling, and taught Samuel how to pray in response.

How do we hear God's voice? How will you hear the voice of the Lord? Will you hear an audible voice? No. Will you experience a strange feeling? No. God's voice will be heard when several things happen:-

(1) Suddenly, you understand what you hear from the Bible! That is, you *really* understand it, not just the facts about people and places (as if it were a school history or geography lesson), but you realise what God is saying about your sin and your need of a Saviour. You understand that the Lord has done something to save you from hell. You understand that you must be converted, changed, and brought to know Him. Has the *meaning* (the *message*) of the Bible dawned on you yet?

(2) Then, you not only understand, but a very special feeling grips you – you realise that *all this is true*. (Sometimes people are quite taken aback and overwhelmed by the awesome realisation that the Bible is *God* speaking.) You no longer think that the Bible is just a religious book which you need not take too seriously. You are certain that it is true, and that its message is serious. You *must* do something about it.

(3) In addition, what God says about your sin – all those lies, tempers, selfish deeds, etc – now makes you feel very ashamed! Previously, no matter what you heard in Sunday School (or what anyone said to you about your bad behaviour) it did not bother you much. But now your conscience is really troubled, and you feel that you are a sinner. You want to be forgiven. When God speaks to us, He touches our hearts and shows us our need of forgiveness, and we become humble people seeking His help.

(4) You also realise that God will deal *personally* with *you*! You say to yourself, 'This message is to *me*. I can be saved. Jesus suffered and died to save a person like me, and if I come to Him, He *will* forgive me, receive me, and make Himself known to me.' Suddenly you feel sure that God is not only real, but He is speaking to you, and calling you to repent and trust Him, and give your life to Him. There may be a great battle in your heart because you still want to carry on with some of your sins, but you cannot turn away, because God is watching you and calling you in His mercy. It becomes a personal matter!

How should we answer God's call? Remind the class of the short, simple and ideal prayer which Eli taught Samuel: *Speak,*

Lord, for Thy servant is listening.

(a) **Speak, Lord.** These two words show that Samuel realised Who was speaking to him, and he was glad and honoured. He wanted to humbly and quietly listen to the Lord. He certainly did not answer back, argue with God or change the subject. When we seek the Lord we accept everything that He says in His Word, the Bible. We believe the Lord.

> *O give me Samuel's ear!*
> *The open ear, O Lord,*
> *Alive and quick to hear*
> *Each whisper of Thy Word;*
> *Like him to answer at Thy call,*
> *And to obey Thee first of all.*

(b) **For Thy servant is listening.** In these words Samuel gave himself to the Lord to be His servant, and promised to listen and obey. We must do exactly the same when we come to the Lord. Without this response no one can ever be a *real* Christian. We say to God, 'I believe what the Bible says about me and my sin. I believe that the Lord Jesus loves me and came into the world to die in my place. From now onwards I will live to obey Thy commands, and to be Thy willing servant. I believe that I must be born again; given a new start. Lord, forgive me, and receive me, and convert my soul.'

Something so wonderful happened to Samuel that night that he lay and wondered at it. The Lord had called *him* by name, and he had responded. Previously he had lived in the house of the Lord (the Tabernacle), but something had been missing. He had not actually known the Lord for himself, but now he did, and it made all the difference! The Lord had spoken, and Samuel had talked with Him.

The test. Explain to your class that this is what shows us whether or not we are Christians. Do we *know* the Lord? Jesus said that eternal life is to know God *(John 17.3)*. He also warned that on the day of judgement He would have to send away many proud, religious people who claimed to have done great things in His name, saying to them, *I never KNEW you (Matthew 7.23)*. Discuss with the children what 'knowing' means. We know our closest friends in a special way. We recognise their voices, we visit their homes, and we know their likes and dislikes. Draw lessons from these. (a) A Christian speaks with the Lord (prays) and recognises His voice. (b) The Lord Jesus said that He and His Father make Their home with those who love Him and obey Him (*John 14.23*). (c) A Christian longs to please the Lord and to avoid all those things which He hates.

Apply these practical tests to the class. However many years of Sunday School experience they can boast, however good their parents and teachers, however successful they are at knowing about the Lord, the all-important questions remain: Do they yet know the Lord for themselves? Do they just 'say prayers' or do they speak with the Lord? Does He live with them day by day? Do they love Him more than anything else or anyone else? Do they want to please and obey Him? Summarise the main points of the lesson. In what four ways does the Lord speak to us, calling us to Himself? How must we pray in response?

The People Demand a King (90)

1 Samuel 7.15-17; 8; 9; 10.1-2 and 17-25; 12.1-5

Aim: To persuade the children (as Samuel did the Israelites) of the great folly of rejecting the Lord, and to highlight God's patience and love to a rebellious people.

Teachers' Introduction

This lesson and the one that follows are part of one narrative. In the first we deal with the decision of the Israelites to demand a king. In the second we follow the rise and fall of Saul, who first held this office. This is probably the most useful division of the subject matter, but individual teachers, and especially those with younger classes, may wish to divide the two lessons at another point.

Lesson Outline

Illustrate graphically the Bible proverb — *Pride goeth before destruction, and an haughty spirit before a fall (Proverbs 16.18, AV).* Either show the children a picture of a proud fool who refuses to heed all warnings falling over a cliff edge, or use a short spoken illustration. Once the children see the point, change the subject to the *spiritual* fool. God's rule is that if we grow too proud to acknowledge Him and respond to Him we shall suffer calamity. This applies to all human life, both individuals and nations, rich and poor.

Open the lesson by telling the class that our next two lessons will provide real-life examples which show how true God's wise advice proves to be. We shall discover what happened when first a nation, and secondly a young man, became too proud to respect the Lord and His ways. Point out that these chapters were not written just to record the history of old-time Israel, but so that *we* should learn very important lessons for our lives (*1 Corinthians 10.11*).

God's good ruler. Tell the class how Samuel had grown up to be a prophet, a priest and a judge-leader of God's people, now settled in their promised land. The people had much for which to be thankful. Unlike the corrupt rulers of the surrounding nations, Samuel had devoted his life — from his childhood call — to the service of God and His people. Not only had he tirelessly visited the major cities to administer justice in his office as judge (*1 Samuel 7.15-17*), but he had also run the Temple services and sacrifices as priest, and on top of all that, had delivered messages from the Lord in his role as prophet. All these tasks he had performed with the humble spirit of a servant, and not as a haughty king. The people agreed that he had never oppressed them, never accepted bribes and never taken advantage of his office (*1 Samuel 12.1-5*). Power had not corrupted him at all, as it does so many rulers, for Samuel lived in deep respect of the Lord and His standards.

Describe then the foolishness of the Israelites as they became dissatisfied with this form of government (called *theocracy*) which God had provided for them. It was free, it was fair, it was effective and it gave them *godly* leadership.

Discontented and ungrateful. Adam and Eve lived in paradise, and yet became discontented and rebellious, forfeiting their paradise for Satan's untested promise of 'freedom'. In a similar manner the people of Israel now approached the ageing Samuel and demanded a king (*1 Samuel 8.5*). They did not care that their ungrateful request would wound and hurt the man to whom they owed so much. Point out to the class that sin is always unkind and selfish.

(1) A FARMER'S BOY

(2) CROWNED KING

(3) OVERTAKEN BY PRIDE

VICIOUS BEHAVIOUR (5)

DESPERATE MEASURES (6)

SUICIDE (7)

DESPISES GOD'S WORD
(4)
DESPISES GOD'S WORD

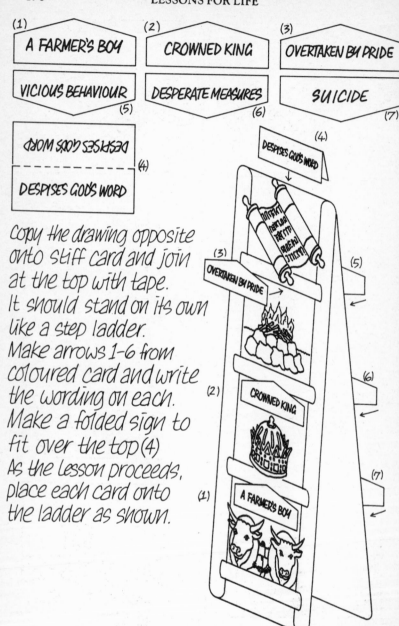

Copy the drawing opposite onto stiff card and join at the top with tape.
It should stand on its own like a step ladder.
Make arrows 1-6 from coloured card and write the wording on each.
Make a folded sign to fit over the top (4)
As the lesson proceeds, place each card onto the ladder as shown.

VA 10 – Visual Aid for use with Lessons 90 and 91 on Saul.

Remind them, as God told Samuel (*1 Samuel 8.7-8*), that their demand was typical of rebellious men and women. Ever since the time when Israel had been saved by God from Egypt, instead of being grateful, they had been trying out new gods, and behaving as if the Lord was a cruel taskmaster.

Neither has this behaviour towards God changed down the course of history. Even though the Lord has demonstrated His love and mercy in the most costly and tender way (through the giving and the death of His own dear Son on Calvary's cross) people still continue to follow any religion, philosophy, or lifestyle which is against God, as though the true God was an undesirable and unreasonable tyrant! Even little children run away from Him, His love and His commands.

God provides a king. Remind the class that God never forces loyalty and obedience on unwilling subjects. He allowed Adam and Eve the freedom to disobey His commands. He also acceded to the demands of the Israelites. They cried out for a king. Instead of appreciating the benefits of being different, they clamoured to be like the other nations around (*1 Samuel 8.19-20*). Ask your class: are they the same — always wanting to be 'in with the crowd' whether for good or bad? The Israelites only had eyes for the glory and the glamour of a *worldly* king. They wanted to exchange the King of Heaven for an *earthly* king.

Samuel warned them of the bitter consequences. He graphically outlined the cost of such a monarchy, reminding them that their kings would be greedy for manpower and money, servants and taxes (*1 Samuel 8.11-17*). But since the people were adamant, the Lord instructed His servant to appoint a king for them. For a while all seemed to go well, but in next week's lesson we shall see how things began to go wrong, both for the new king and the nation.

A warning for us. Summon all your powers of persuasion to warn the children about the dangers of rejecting their Maker and Saviour. History teaches us over and over again that rebelling against the God of the Bible only brings the high costs of loss, pain, suffering and oppression (a point illustrated by the Lord Jesus in His parable of the Prodigal Son). It is proof of the deeply rebellious state of our hearts that by nature we refuse to listen to any of these arguments and rush headlong down to hell, rather than seek forgiveness and mercy from the God Who still mercifully invites us to return to Him and His ways.

'God save the king!' Tell the class briefly that Saul, a young man from the least significant family of the smallest tribe of Israel (*1 Samuel 9.21*), was anointed by Samuel to be the first king of Israel while on a routine search for his father's asses. At first he was overwhelmed by the great privileges and blessings bestowed on him, and on the occasion of his first presentation to the people hid himself (*1 Samuel 10.22*). As soon as he was discovered, the people received this young man, head and shoulders taller than everyone else, as their king. For the first time in history the cry went up, *God save the king!*

Before sending them to their homes, Samuel laid down the guide lines for their new constitution under a king, and wrote it in a book (*1 Samuel 10.25*). Saul was not left to struggle alone in his new role. Samuel, now old and experienced at ruling the people of Israel, prepared the way for the new king. So it was that Samuel, gracious to the end, handed over his powers as ruler and judge (but not as priest and prophet) to Saul. Despite their ingratitude towards him, Samuel assured the people of Israel that he would continue to pray for them and instruct them. His advice was — *Only fear the Lord and serve Him in truth with all your heart; for consider what great things He has done for you (1 Samuel 12.24).*

Close by assuring your class that, whatever course they take in life, *you* will continue to pray for them. Urge them to remember always what you have taught them about the Lord and the wonderful things He has done for them, so that they will be saved from the kind of spiritual disasters which were soon to overtake Saul and the people of Israel.

Visual Aid

Begin the use of VA 10 (see pages 196-197) which depicts Saul's rise to power.

The Rise and Fall of a Proud King (91)

1 Samuel 13.1-15; 28 and 31

Aim: To help the class recognise the ugliness of pride and the tragic consequences when it carries people away from the Lord.

Teachers' Introduction

The visual aid for this lesson will be particularly helpful in summarising the main events of Saul's life and in making a vivid and practical application. It pictures the various events as steps, first up, and then down, a ladder. King Saul is an example of someone who did not know when to stop. Not content with God's promotion from being a farmer's boy to being king of Israel, he experienced a tragic fall, and so provides a warning for all.

Lesson Outline

Up: success. (To introduce the lesson refer to Saul's selection as king, from the previous lesson, using the suggested visual aid with its labels – 'A Farmer's Boy' and 'Crowned King'.) Soon after his coronation, King Saul was exercising a powerful rule, successfully leading the Israelites out to battle. Sadly this led him to become 'puffed up' and proud. He began to enjoy the sweet savour of applause, and gave himself the credit which rightly belonged to the Lord.

Up: overtaken by pride, despises God's Word. Explain to the class that since childhood Saul had been trained to respect the awesome task of the priests in his nation. The tribe of Levi was especially set apart by the Lord for this sacred work. Their way of life, their special clothing, and their functions in the Tabernacle, all marked them out as those who were exclusively authorised by God to lead the worship of the people. Only they were allowed to offer up sacrifices. This was to teach the people: (1) how holy God is, and how unfit the people were to approach Him; (2) that the Lord must be approached only in the precise way which He had laid down; and (3) that only God could arrange a sacrifice to take away sin.

Imagine then Samuel's horror when, having been delayed, he arrived at the scene of a battle only to discover that Saul had brushed God's rules aside, and had offered up a sacrifice himself. Instead of humbly turning to the Lord in a moment of crisis, the young king had shown great arrogance and treated God's instructions with contempt. Saul sneered at all that he had been taught, and decided that he was worthy and entitled to take over the function of God's appointed priest. This act betrayed Saul's state of heart, showing the extent to which pride and self-esteem had taken hold of him.

Danger zone. Warn the children that this attitude is the one which leads to every other sin. Eve fell into sin as soon as she believed Satan's suggestion, *Has God said?* She said to herself, 'Does it matter what God says? Why should I have to obey?' We are all inclined to think like this. We behave as if we are in no way related to God; as though we owe Him nothing, His commands do not matter, and we know better.

This point is particularly relevant to children. If they have grown up in the atmosphere of a Sunday School or a Christian home they soon come to the crossroads of life where they must take one road or the other. Will they follow Samuel's example of obedience, or will they be like Saul and rebel against the Lord's commands? Explain that Saul's course of action was disastrous. He offended Samuel, but worse, he offended the Lord and betrayed the fact that he was unworthy to hold the high office with which he had been entrusted.

Down: despised God's Word – again. Before long Saul was to act in an even more outrageous way. He was given precise instructions by Samuel. God had decreed that Saul must utterly destroy the Amalekites, who had treated the homeless Israelites with great cruelty as they journeyed from Egypt to Canaan. This was *not* to be a battle where the victorious side could help themselves to the rich possessions of their defeated enemy. God would enable the Israelites to win because He would be punishing the Amalekites and destroying all their possessions.

This would serve as a demonstration to all of His anger toward sinful people, and naturally the demonstration would mean nothing if the people were allowed to take home the 'spoils'. It would be like a judge sending a thief to prison, and then taking for his own personal use the things which the thief had stolen. However, when Samuel arrived at the scene of battle he was again dismayed. He heard animals (seized from the enemy) bleating and found that Agag, the Amalekite king, was alive. Saul had blatantly disobeyed.

Sin exposed. (Visual aid note: for this most important point, a large label – 'Sin exposed!' may be fixed over the Scripture scroll on the 'down' side of the ladder.) When Saul's sin was uncovered by Samuel he responded in three ways:-

(a) He used deceit. At first Saul greeted Samuel as if all were perfectly in order, hoping Samuel would overlook the fact that his instructions had not been obeyed. He tried a cover-up! (*1 Samuel 15.13.*) How often we try this ploy! We know we have done wrong things, but we behave as though nothing has happened and hope to gloss over our deeds. However, when we stand before God's judgement throne no pretence will fool the Lord.

(b) He put the blame elsewhere. Next Saul blamed the people (v 15). This ploy was first used by Adam when he blamed Eve for his sin. How often do we blame our circumstances, other people, etc, for our wrongdoing?

(c) He made hopeless excuses. Next Saul made the excuse that the animals which had been taken were intended as a sacrifice for the Lord (v 15). (Point out that this was probably a lie as well as an excuse.) But the Lord wanted *obedience*, not sacrifice (v 22). Explain that God never accepts bribes in exchange for overlooking sin. We cannot live evil lives and expect that He will accept some penance as payment. People have the idea that churches are here to *sell* forgiveness (and indeed many have done that, but against God's will). Some rich people have suddenly given away huge sums of money to a good cause when they have realised that death is near. They have hoped that this might please God.

Tell the class that the Lord looks for hearts that genuinely listen to Him and trust Him. He will not be hoodwinked by anything. Tell the class God's verdict on sin. Samuel spelled out the consequences – *The Lord has torn the kingdom of Israel from you today, and has given it to your neighbour* (v 28).

Down: vicious behaviour. So it was that Saul became a vicious, evil-tempered man overcome by terrible moods, and capable of turning even against those who respected and served him most. He forced Samuel, who had great regard for him, to retreat from him. Soon his kingdom was torn by civil war, and threatened by enemies around.

Down: desperate measures. This tragic biography closes with Saul, driven to despair, secretly seeking the advice of a witch (*1 Samuel 28.7-14*), a drastic measure for a king who had outlawed all such practices from his kingdom on pain of death. Finally, Saul suffered disastrous loss on the battlefield and decided to take his own life (*1 Samuel 31.1-6*). (Note visual aid label – 'Suicide'.)

The consequences of pride. Simply but earnestly draw the children's attention to the lesson to be learned from Saul, a foolish man, who was given great and wonderful opportunities, but who threw them all away. As he rejected God's Word the success he had been granted slowly began to crack and disintegrate until it finally collapsed in disaster. How wise the Bible is in predicting that pride is followed by a fall!

Warn the class against believing the cruel and lying propaganda of this world which tells them life without God is free and wonderful. Explain that it is only the Christian life which gives liberty and real happiness. Ask the class to observe the real lives they see around them and to notice how often nations and individual people resemble Saul. How quickly proud empires have fallen! And yet countless people proudly reject the Lord and ignore His commands. They think they know better. But before long disappointment and tragedy sets in. Problems crop up on all sides. Unhappiness and despair ought to lead people to seek the Lord, but many defy the Lord to the end, and then risk hell, rather than ask for His pardon and forgiveness. Urge your class to learn this lesson from Saul and not to repeat the experiment in their own lives. Remind them that *God is opposed to the proud, but gives grace to the humble (James 4.6).*

Visual Aid

Continue the use of VA 10 (see pages 196-197) which depicts Saul's rise, fall and tragic end.

Revision (92)
Judgement or Deliverance

Lesson references and Hebrews 11.31-40

Aim: To review this pageantry of Bible history, not just in terms of its great events, but to divide the characters into two categories, namely: those who lived only for the here-and-now (and suffered the eternal, spiritual consequences), and those who lived by faith and who were blessed by the Lord.

Two categories. The precise form of this lesson will vary with the age of the class and preference of the teacher. Divide the chief characters of the series into two groups: (A) UNBELIEVERS – Achan, the people of Laish, and Saul, and (B) BELIEVERS – Rahab, Gideon, Ruth and Samuel.

(A) Unbelievers. Consider with the children what group (A) had in common. Achan, the greedy thief; Laish, the selfish city; and Saul, the proud king. All were devoted to looking after their own interests as if there were no God and no eternity. They assumed that, even if God did exist, He did not know or care how they behaved. Each ignored His laws and commands. Each wanted a good life *now*, and did whatever they thought would get it for them. Remind or question the class about the events we have learned which prove this to be the case. Also remind the children that people today are the same. This is their view of life: 'I am here to enjoy myself, and to get what I can for myself. If there is a God, what difference does that make? Who is to tell me how I should live?' Then consider what happened to each one of our three examples. Achan was found out and punished. Laish was invaded and conquered. Saul had his kingdom taken from him.

(B) Believers. Now review the second group of people: Rahab, an immoral Canaanite woman; Gideon, a 'commoner' and farmer's son; Ruth, an immigrant widow; and Samuel, a young boy who served in the Lord's Temple. Ask what these all had in common. Explain that the book of *Hebrews* names most of these in a list of people who lived *by faith*. Explain what this means – that they put their trust in the Lord for the forgiveness of their sin, and for the course of their lives. Ask the following questions, and credit or clarify the answers as necessary: –

(1) What did Rahab believe which made her welcome the Israelite spies to Jericho?

(2) What did Gideon do to Baal which proved that he believed there was only one God, the all-powerful, unseen God of Israel?

(3) Why was Ruth (unlike Orpah) prepared to leave her home, her family and her religion to travel to the country of her mother-in-law?

(4) What attitude of heart and mind led to the boy Samuel having the Lord speak to him in a direct and personal way? (He was willing to listen.)

Ask the class the all-important question: Into which category do they fit, group (A) or group (B)? Show them that it concerns you very much, because the outcome was so different for each group.

Judgement for group (A). Achan, the people of Laish, and Saul met with tragic ends. Their unbelief led to their being unprotected from: (i) their guilt, (ii) the dangers of life, and (iii) their own sinful appetites and urges. Counsel the class not to be like Achan by imagining they can hide from God; or like the people of Laish, by imagining there are no spiritual dangers or enemies; or like Saul, by being ruled by pride.

Deliverance for group (B). By contrast, Rahab, Gideon, Ruth and Samuel were delivered from great dangers and difficult situations in *this* life, as well as receiving a safe passage right into Heaven. Their lives were made useful by the Lord here, and they could also look forward to spending eternity with Him. Urge the class to follow their example: to be like Rahab, by responding to God's warnings; to be like Gideon, by obeying God and serving on the Lord's side; to be like Ruth, by trusting themselves into the Lord's wonderful care; and to be like Samuel, by being willing to listen to God, and to obey His call, whenever it comes.

Draw together the strands of this series. What was it that separated the first group from the second? The first group had no faith; they did not see God in their affairs. The second group *had* faith; they lived, *as seeing Him who is unseen* (*Hebrews 11.27*). Remind the class that it is a foolish person who refuses to believe in electricity because it cannot be seen. It is even more foolish to disbelieve and ignore God because He cannot be seen by human eyes. All around us we see evidence of God's power and love in His creation. In this series we have learned about those who experienced His goodness in their own lives. Urge the class to do the same.

Lessons for Life, books *1-4*

Lessons for Life 2 is the second to be published of four books of Sunday School lessons designed to cover a four-year syllabus. The third and fourth books (now in preparation) follow the same format, consisting of lessons which have proved successful in Sunday Schools over many years, now revised by the author. The contents of each book are as follows: —

Lessons for Life 1 (lessons 1-46)

Miracles Demonstrating Jesus' Power (Mark's Gospel — Part I)
The Lord's saving power seen in His power over nature, death, the devil, human need and illness (5 lessons)

In the Beginning (Genesis — Part I)
The truth about God, creation and the fall, with the earliest salvation testimonies (6 lessons)

Opposition to Jesus (Mark's Gospel — Part II)
Examples of key sins — prejudice, pride, hardness, hate, etc — seen in the Lord's opponents, and to be repented of by all (6 lessons)

Highlights from the Conversion and Preaching Journeys of Paul (Acts — Part I)
Evangelistic lessons from the life (and converts) of the apostle (8 lessons)

God's Great Plans (Genesis — Part II)
Character studies from Abraham to Joseph showing the power and goodness of God towards His people (12 lessons)

The 'I AM' Sayings of the Lord Jesus (John's Gospel)
Exalting the Saviour through His own great metaphors — the Living Water, the Bread of Life, etc (9 lessons)

Lessons for Life 2 (lessons 47-92)

The Christian Pilgrimage — Salvation from Sin's Slavery (Exodus — Joshua — Part I)
The journey from Egypt to Sinai (8 lessons)

People Who Followed Jesus (Luke's Gospel — Part I)
Lessons on Christian conversion and its chief characteristics (11 lessons)

The Christian Pilgrimage — Pictures of Salvation and Heaven (Exodus — Joshua — Part II)
The journey continues from Sinai to Jordan (6 lessons)

Gospel Appeals in the Saviour's Parables (Luke's Gospel — Part II)
Teaching the consequences of sin and the only way of escape (11 lessons)

Judgement and Deliverance (Joshua — 1 Samuel)
Examples and warnings for all, from Rahab to Saul (10 lessons)

Lessons for Life 3 (lessons 93-138)
(in preparation)

Gains and Losses in Following Jesus (Mark's Gospel – Part III)
Repentance, faith and conversion, and their alternatives (8 lessons)

Great Differences (1 Samuel – 1 Kings)
Contrasts drawn from the life of David and Solomon to illustrate conversion and the believer's privileges (12 lessons)

Early Reactions to the Apostles' Message (Acts – Part II)
Various categories of hearer and the Holy Spirit's work in their lives (6 lessons)

Sin and Its Cure (1 and 2 Kings – Elijah and Elisha)
The nature of sin and its punishment, with God's remedy graphically presented (8 lessons)

The Saviour Comes and Begins His Work (Matthew's Gospel – Part I)
A chronological account of the life and teaching of the Lord highlighting His attributes and saving purpose (12 lessons)

Lessons for Life 4 (lessons 139-184)
(in preparation)

The Word of God (Amos to Jeremiah)
The Bible authenticated in history and in transformed lives

The Life, Death and Resurrection of the Lord Jesus (Matthew's Gospel – Part II)
Continuing the chronological account of the life and teaching of the Lord

Character Studies from Daniel, Ezra and Nehemiah
The transforming work of grace and its dramatic results

How God Fits Us for Heaven
The steps of salvation explained from Romans and applied to young people today

The Lord's Ten Great Commandments
The 'schoolmaster' to lead us to Christ and the way of safety and fulfilment

Lessons for Life users may wish to use the take-home leaflets (also in preparation) to accompany the lessons each week. These are entitled: *Lessons for Life Bible Learning Course.* They feature an outline picture for colouring by children, questions and a hymn verse related to the lesson, and suggested passages for personal Bible reading for the ensuing week. Other helps, such as visual aid materials, are also in course of preparation. Enquiries for take-home leaflets, and news of other materials should be made to:– Lessons for Life, Metropolitan Tabernacle, Elephant & Castle, London SE1 6SD.